A PENGUIN SPECIAL

PERSECUTION EAST AND WEST

Cosmas Desmond was born in the East End of London in 1935 and educated at Cardinal Vaughan Grammar School. He entered the Order of Friars Minors (Franciscans) in 1952 and was ordained in 1959. He then went to South Africa as a missionary where he worked among Zulu people until 1968. He became involved with the government's African 'resettlement' programme when the people on his mission station received eviction notices because it was a 'white' area. He undertook research on 'resettlement' throughout the country and his findings were published in *The Discarded People* (Penguin, 1971). He subsequently lectured and wrote on this subject and other aspects of government policy until he was banned and placed under house-arrest in 1971. After his release in 1975 he resumed his research and writing, focusing particularly on African unemployment. In 1972 he left the priesthood, having been told that the Order would not support him if he insisted on embarrassing the government by deliberately breaking his restriction order. He returned to England in 1978, as he thought there was no longer any role for a white person to play in the struggle in South Africa.

He was appointed Director of the British Section of Amnesty International in June 1979 and was dismissed in March 1981 after 'a protracted dispute by two members of staff, who refused for personal reasons to accept a restructuring of the office, and internal conflict and confusion about the direction the movement should take'.

His other publications include *Christians or Capitalists? Religion and Politics in South Africa*, *Limehill Revisited: A Case-study of the Longer-term Effects of Resettlement* and *South African Unemployment: A Black Picture* (co-editor).

He lives in London with his wife and three sons.

COSMAS DESMOND

PERSECUTION
EAST AND WEST

HUMAN RIGHTS,
POLITICAL PRISONERS AND AMNESTY

PENGUIN BOOKS

Penguin Books Ltd, Harmondsworth, Middlesex, England
Penguin Books, 625 Madison Avenue, New York, New York 10022, U.S.A.
Penguin Books Australia Ltd, Ringwood, Victoria, Australia
Penguin Books Canada Ltd, 2801 John Street, Markham, Ontario, Canada L3R 1B4
Penguin Books (N.Z.) Ltd, 182–190 Wairau Road, Auckland 10, New Zealand.

First published 1983

Made and printed in Great Britain by
Richard Clay (The Chaucer Press) Ltd, Bungay, Suffolk
Filmset in Monophoto Sabon by
Northumberland Press Ltd, Gateshead

CONTENTS

PREFACE

In 1961 Penguin published Peter Benenson's *Persecution 1961* as part of his 'Appeal for Amnesty', which directly led to the founding of Amnesty International. In 1981 Peter Walker, who was then Fund-raising and Publicity Officer for the British Section of Amnesty, approached Penguin with the suggestion that they should publish another book to mark the twenty-first anniversary of Amnesty. Penguin agreed, and it was thought appropriate that an assessment of the organization's work should be written by a former prisoner of conscience, who was also the current Director of the British Section. This is not that book, since I also became an ex-Director. I am grateful, nevertheless, to Peter Walker for the original suggestion and to Neil Middleton of Penguin for agreeing that I should write on a broader theme. The reader is not likely to be given the impression that this is in any way an official Amnesty publication, so no formal disclaimer is required.

In my last book I neglected to thank the South African government for putting me under house-arrest, thus giving me time to read and reflect and so to be able to produce the book. I do not wish to make a similar oversight this time. I should, therefore, like to record my thanks to those members of the British Section of Amnesty International who, in working so assiduously to engineer my departure, gave me another opportunity of writing, which I prefer to being a bureaucrat. I trust they will spend a similar amount of energy in providing General Pinochet and Piet Botha with time for reflection by relieving them of the cares of government.

I am also most grateful to Peter Benenson for his hospitality and for the time he devoted to a couple of long discussions. He is not, of course, in any way responsible for the conclusions I have drawn from those discussions or for the use I have made of the material he kindly loaned me. I have not had the opportunity of asking his opinion of what I have written; however, I did find him in ready agreement with my preliminary criticism of the course Amnesty has taken. The criticisms I make are in no sense an adverse reflection on his original vision, which I consider to have been wholly admirable but seriously misunderstood and misinterpreted in practice.

The majority of the staff of the British Section, as readers with a memory for ephemeral press reports might recall, were opposed to my removal from office. These, together with other Amnesty members, very generously presented me with an electric typewriter, which eased the burdensome task of my wife and my sister-in-law, Marguerite Desmond, in typing the final draft; my sincere thanks to the donors and to the users. I am also grateful to my former secretary, Sheila Field, now also a former staff member, who was always prepared to be pestered about obtaining publications and information; and to Derek Roebuck, Amnesty's Head of Research, for some very helpful conversations, which he held in his personal capacity and which do not make him in any way responsible for anything I have written.

Finally, I thank my wife; for once it is not a cliché to add 'but for whom this book would not have been written'. It was she who finally persuaded me not to worry about the wranglings in Amnesty, and to write. She also maintained what I considered to be a quite unfounded belief: that I would complete the book in time. My apologies to Timothy, Christopher and Nicholas for restricting their freedom of movement; and my thanks for their co-operation.

INTRODUCTION

Africa and Amnesty

This is not an academic work on the nature of human rights or on the philosophy of oppression, though both subjects are touched upon. Nor is it simply a description of all the horrors of oppression throughout the world. Any need of such a descriptive account is met more adequately by Amnesty International's Annual Reports and other publications than it could be by me. It is, rather, a personal reflection on some of the questions that have arisen as a result of two very different experiences of being involved in the struggle against oppression and in the defence of human rights.

It is a mixture of hard facts and personal reminiscences, a little philosophy, and even a bit of theology; all of which go to make up a polemic rather than a dispassionate thesis. I write as a Christian and as a socialist who is implacably hostile to capitalism as a politico-economic system and to the values on which it is based. I am convinced, not as a matter of belief or theory, but because of my experience of the extreme lengths to which capitalists in South Africa have gone to give expression to those values, that there can be no question of compromise with them. I am, however, only a little less hostile to the Soviet Union's practice of socialism. This does not mean that I think everyone is out of step except me; it simply means that I do not believe in imposing predetermined limits on human progress. Socialists and Christians share a conviction of the perfectability of humanity; I, therefore, have it in double measure. I am not a doctrinaire Marxist, which in any event is, I think, according to Marx's own method, a contradiction in terms. Marx provides useful analytical tools, not dogmas, and I have no belief in his infallibility. I do, however, believe that Marx was, above all, a moralizer. His most ardent supporters and his most violent opponents would probably be at one in denying this; the former would claim that he was not concerned at all with morals, the latter that he was immoral. He did, however, true to his background, continue the Jewish prophetic tradition of thundering against injustice. In his efforts to rid the world of injustice he tried to provide an answer to all the world's problems. Not surprisingly, he failed; but his merit lies in the fact that he tried and that he succeeded in making a large contribution. His followers do him a disservice in canonizing not only him, but his 'answers'. As they say in Mozambique and Angola, 'A luta continua' – 'the struggle continues'.

While I would lay no claim to, or (depending on the reader's point of view) accept no blame for, being an intellectual, I do believe that one's head can be put to a better use than being a battering ram to knock down brick walls. I do not raise questions as an intellectual exercise, but only because, even though some may appear a little abstruse, I have been convinced, mainly through failures, that unless they are answered to one's own satisfaction – if not to that of the armchair academics – one is led to frustration, despair and even self-destruction by meaningless failure. Battering one's own or anybody else's head against a brick wall does not get one very far. Much energy is wasted by people making frenzied attempts to find ways of getting somewhere even through brick walls, when either they are not too sure of where it is they want to go or, deep down, they do not really believe they can ever get there. There is some wisdom for them in the advice the peasant gave to the traveller: if you want to get to the place in question you shouldn't be starting from here.

If you want to understand and to combat oppression, the best place is to start with oppression at its source, rather than with an abstract ideal about man or society or human rights based on preconceived principles or, even worse, on legalistic formulations. An ideal is, as I shall argue, essential if one is to do anything about the fate of one's fellow human beings and hence also about one's own. But an *abstract* ideal is a barrier, rather than a spur, to the practical expression of an ideal. The basis of a practical and attainable ideal is experience and commitment, as opposed to knowledge and concern. I personally found the former in South Africa and the latter in Amnesty International; in South Africa I also found humour and hope.

Effective action against oppression depends on one's experience of it, which gives rise to a commitment to overcoming it; understanding comes later. It is not possible first to understand oppression and then to decide to do something about it. It is not necessary to travel thousands of miles to gain this experience; oppression, like charity, begins at home and is, I shall further argue, indivisible. My own path took me through South Africa, but I am sure I would have reached the same point via Margaret Thatcher's Britain. And the point is the conviction that a radical transformation of human beings in society is not only an obvious necessity, but is also possible if, and only if, we abandon the Western individualist views and the attendant reformist practices. We can then commit ourselves to a socialist, which I would say is also the Christian, pursuit of the common destiny of mankind, idealistic and even romantic as that may sound.

The individualistic approach might seem more realistic, but it is its realism which is manifested in the present reality of oppression. If that is all there is to reality, we might as well give up all hope. Those who are 'concerned' about oppression have not, and cannot have, any hope that the world can be radically changed; oppression is the reality, all they can do is be concerned. But the more one experiences oppression the more grounds one has for such hope. If two thirds of the world's population can suffer in the way they do and yet retain much of the human dignity that has been lost in the other third, they are also capable of raising the level of that dignity for all of us. People suffering and struggling together are surely more likely to be the bearers of a better future than those who are planning together to decide whether they need the power to annihilate everybody ten times over or whether once would be enough; even though, or rather because it is the latter who are 'advanced' and who have the technology and resources to solve the world's economic problems. We do not have an economic problem, we have a *human* one. And one that can be solved by the full realization of the human potential now hidden under a mass of oppression – a potential which people are prevented from recognizing because they see oppression as the only reality. Such a 'realistic' view cannot even conceive of the possibility of oppression being transformed into human freedom.

This brings us back to the need for raising fundamental questions instead of assuming that we already have the answers. Western 'answers', which are based on a traditional liberal, individualistic philosophy of man and society (it does not consider man *in* society), have not begun – nor can they begin to solve, or to reach an understanding of the problem of oppression. We know from experience that they *have* not. If we reflect on that experience we discover that they *cannot*. Understanding does not come from a study of the facts. 'To grasp the meaning of a human fact is to grasp it in itself and in oneself', Leopold Senghor quotes Picon as saying. It does not suffice, he himself continues, 'to see it, to dissect it, to weigh it, even if one has the most perfect precision instruments. One must also touch it, penetrate it from inside – so to speak – and finger it. To know a human fact, psychological, or social, no longer means (as it does in traditional Western philosophy) to investigate it with the aid of statistics and graphs, but to live it: like the white man who, to understand the situation of Negro Americans, blackened his skin with a chemical product and worked as a Negro shoeshine boy' (*On African Socialism*, p. 71).

I do not claim in any way to speak for the oppressed, nor am I suggesting that I went to South Africa to become a 'Negro shoe-shine boy'. However, I do necessarily think and write out of my own comparatively limited experience of oppression, which I first became consciously aware of in South Africa. One's understanding of oppression does not necessarily increase in proportion with one's experience of it, nor does it make one an expert – certainly not of the technical kind who are engaged in the human rights industry. My own involvement is comparatively limited in so far as my personal experience as a victim is concerned. I was not imprisoned for years and years, I was not tortured and, perhaps to the chagrin of those who made the threats, I was not extra-judicially executed. But during my eighteen years in what is probably the most systematically oppressive country in the world I also experienced the effects of oppression on and with others. The limitations to my experience in this respect are only those imposed by time and, much more significantly, by the fact that I was white. Being banned and put under house-arrest makes a white person only a little more physically restricted than all Africans are, but at least it thereby gives one some understanding of their experience of oppression. For that reason, although the life of a banned person has been well described as a 'half-life; a twilight existence, the life of a social leper', it is also, or was for me, much more than that. For some it can be a soul-destroying experience; not so much because of the physical restrictions, which one can learn to live with, especially if you happen to have spent seven years being cooped up in a seminary; but because of the frustration of being unable to be actively involved, because of the lack of communication and stimulation. The constant tension is in not knowing when 'they' are going to come – any noise which awakens you during the night is 'them' (six years later it still is!), and if one is honest one must admit, I suppose, at least a tinge of fear at what the consequences of their arrival will be.

I found it, however, a happier and more fulfilling experience than my life both in the seminary and at Amnesty. (In the latter case the explanation might be the one given by an Amnesty council member, who considered that the pressure of working for Amnesty was greater than any pressure that I may have been subject to in South Africa!) This happiness did not stem from a masochistic pleasure in being a martyr; though there was perhaps a sadistic delight in being a thorn in the flesh of such a government. More important was the awareness that, even if only in a small way, one was part of a much larger struggle. This more than compensated for any hardship. In any event, as I wrote when I was released, 'I found it boring, irritating and frustrating, but any hardship I had to endure was nothing compared to that of a man like Joe Morolong. His world is a small area of bare veld

north of Vryburg; he is his own jailer in the silence of a tiny hut; he has no
access to any of the amenities which even a banned person takes for granted
in Johannesburg.' I never met Morolong, but throughout the period of my
own house-arrest the knowledge of his existence served as a continuous
reminder that, even as a banned person, I was still privileged. I developed
almost a guilt complex about him. The Press was full of stories about me,
people wrote to me from all over the world, Amnesty International adopted
me, but few people had even heard of Joe Morolong. When his restriction
orders were renewed he was no longer alive to serve them.

My guilt feelings were also aroused when I heard of the death in prison
of a man whose name at present eludes me. When I publicly and deliberately
violated my restriction orders by going to a church service as an act of
protest, no action was taken against me. He went quite innocently since,
being illiterate in English, he did not know the terms of his restriction order;
yet he was arrested and sent to prison, because he also had other suspended
sentences; but he was black and was going to an independent African
Church. When people talk of how terrible the practice of banning and
house-arrest without trial is, it is Joe Morolong's experience rather than my
own which comes to mind. His was much worse, but at least my experience
enables me to understand his. One does not have to have exactly the same
experience in order to understand the experience of others, but one needs
some common experience. A parent, for example, does not need to lose a
child in order to understand what such a loss means to another parent, but
he or she needs to be a parent.

Had my restriction orders been renewed I would doubtless still be part
of the struggle in South Africa. I could cope with being a privileged house-
arrested person, but not with being a privileged, though harassed and
threatened, 'free' one. I did, both before and after my period of house-arrest,
have the opportunity of getting as deeply 'inside' the experience of other
forms of oppression as was possible for me as a white person. But this did
not happen by means of the graphs and statistics on African unemployment
and 'resettlement' which I helped to produce and which I think were worth
producing. The experience of others can rub off on to you only if you get
close enough to them as people; the facts about them are not enough.

My first real awareness of oppression in South Africa, as opposed to the
somewhat detached concern of the pastor for the needs of his flock, came
not from the knowledge of the evil of the whole apartheid system – or even
of the 'resettlement' programme in particular. It came when a few people
who were close friends were directly affected by that programme. I was
certainly concerned before: who could not be when faced daily with the

sight of children literally starving to death because their fathers, who were migrant workers, could not afford to keep themselves (and possibly a companion and even a second family) in the city and to send money home; or because the whole family was 'tied' to a white farmer who paid them £3 a year? But I was not aware of what it all meant in either political or human terms. I was only an observer, a concerned and sympathetic one, but still an observer. It was only because of those few friends that I was able to see the 'resettlement' of two million people, the daily arrests of thousands of Africans, the mass starvation, not only as facts but as human facts. The fact that a person is tortured to death in prison is enough to shock and anger anybody, but when it happens to somebody with whom you were having a drink a few weeks before, you have a different experience of that and of every other death in detention; one cannot imagine what it means to those who have lost one or even several relatives in this way.

But there is not only an opportunity for experiencing suffering in an oppressive country. One experiences the humanity of the oppressed more than the inhumanity of the oppressors. This is particularly evident in the bearing and obvious freedom of accused people in political trials. Aelred Stubbs, in his book on Steve Biko, describes his attendance at a trial of some SASO (South African Students Organization) members with a nun. The nine entered singing a freedom song; it was the police who had 'set, tense, joyless and, yes, frightened expressions'. Then 'at the end of the song, a roar from the nine, "*Amandla*", and from the crowd a forest of arms shooting up and the deafening response of "*Ngawethu*" ("strength ... is ours"). "There is not much doubt who's in power here, is there?" whispered the little Sister' (p. 182). Note that the slogan, which is now common to all South African liberation groups, does not say 'Power *will be* ours' but 'Power *is* ours'. It is not present just in some sort of inner freedom despite their physical conditions; the rejection of those conditions is in their very being; and *amandla*, 'power' means much more than sheer physical strength.

This is not a romantic notion, nor is it based on such a puerile and basically racist idea as: 'Africans must be happy because they are always singing'. They often sing to make themselves happy – by insulting their white 'bosses' rather than by the music – not because they *are* happy. (And many of them *haven't* got rhythm either.) Whites might not be so enthralled by the primitive chant of the road-gang if they were aware that the words that often accompany the rhythmic swing of the picks are 'God damn the Whites'.

The humanity is shown not only by their resilience to suffering and their determination to resist, but also by the example of people like Lawrence Ndzanga. He and his wife Rita, both trade unionists, were detained by the Security Police in the early hours of the morning and forced to leave their three young children alone in the house. They were detained for seventeen months, during which time they were tortured, brought to trial, acquitted and re-detained without being allowed to leave the court, and finally acquitted again. The first thing he said upon his release after a formal exchange of greetings was, 'What can we do about getting our people unemployment benefits?' He was immediately back into his trade unionist role and was worried about others; he did not say a word about what he had been through. He continued his trade union work until he and Rita were detained again and he died in prison, of 'natural causes'. He was probably not deliberately murdered, but the causes were only 'natural' if it is natural continually to detain and torture people. (On the day I wrote this paragraph I read of Rita being detained yet again.) Amnesty used a picture of Rita at his graveside as a poster because of its emotional impact, but they were both far more than objects of sympathy; they were examples of what human beings can be. The Amnesty candle is a symbol of hope, but it is people like the Ndzangas who keep that flame alive, not an organization, nor even 'concerned' people.

Britain was a more human and community-minded society during the war than it is now, but I would not advocate having another war in order to rediscover those values. Nor am I suggesting that oppression is in any way justified because it gives people the opportunity of showing how human they can be. It shows what they *are*; and what they are is a challenge to what *we* are. Similarly the inhumanity of the oppressors is a challenge. These people are not just victims of inhuman oppression, they are also the bearers of the new humanity.

I could go on and on giving examples of the humanity not just of political leaders, but of ordinary people – mothers in 'resettlement camps' nursing their children dying of typhoid or gastro-enteritis; people supporting the old, the sick, the mentally handicapped and the unemployed in the community, instead of treating them as social outcasts and misfits as the more 'advanced' societies do.

I am not concerned with making an apologia either for my life or for this book. In giving the above account, I simply want to show, firstly, that this book has grown out of a very real experience. To make this point I have touched upon experiences of which I do not normally speak, let alone boast: 'Of the ineffable one does not speak' (Wittgenstein). I do not claim that this experience uniquely equips me to write this book or to be an authority on human rights – or even that it causes me to be more concerned about them than anybody else. But it is part of me and I have not now put any thought of it from my mind in order to concentrate on 'theory'; in reflecting on that experience I have tried to offer an explanation of *human* facts which I already know, in Senghor's sense, to be true. I *know* that sincerity, zeal, dedication, reformism, aid, sympathy and all the other liberal motives for, and expressions of, concern are not enough. And I am convinced that they *cannot* be enough, because they are based on a preconceived idea of the limits of human potential; yet oppressed people are extending those limits all the time. It is necessary, therefore, to reject such preconceived ideas so that we can join in the process of becoming more human ourselves. The knowledge comes from experience; it is only the attempted explanation which comes from reflection. This explanation is given in the hope that it might help a few others to make sense of their experience and even of their failures. Secondly, because of this experience, when I speak of the 'oppressed' I am not thinking of 'a problem' but of real, live, or often dead people. And they are people whom I admire rather than feel sorry for, though I have tried to 'sym-pathize' with them.

I hesitate to mention Steve Biko because, much as he would have dis-approved of it, he has been turned into something of a cult figure, even a plastercast saint, which he certainly did not want to be. Adam Small, the South African black poet, wrote shortly after Biko's death, 'I have no wish to be part of the excesses of white liberal people in response to his death: the accolades that suddenly discovered the "towering" stature of Steve Biko ... I recall that Steve Biko had a sense of humour. He might well have laughed to learn that he was all these magnificent things they are now saying' (*Drum* magazine, November 1977). It is precisely for that reason that I mention him: to illustrate one of the major differences between oppressed people and 'concerned' people, the former can and do laugh, at themselves and at their oppression. The community presided over by Steve Biko at King Williamstown was an oasis of humanity, which was not blighted by the fact that its members were regularly detained; it was noted for its parties. On one occasion where all those present had at least been banned, if not imprisoned, there was an hilarious discussion on how much time each one was 'prepared' to spend in prison and what they would be like when they came out. Steve reckoned that twelve years was enough for him. A few weeks later one of them, Mapetla Mohapi, was killed in prison and Steve Biko was to follow. But, as Adam Small concludes his article, '... without fanfare, without shouting ... Steve Biko is "not dead".' Steve and many other oppressed people would give the same advice to 'concerned' people as Jesus did to the women of Jerusalem: 'Weep not for me, but for yourselves and for your children.'

The other experience on which this book is based is that of being Director of the British Section of Amnesty International; I have also drawn widely on information published by Amnesty. I am not concerned with the history of Amnesty; I have no interest whatsoever in the intrigues which have plagued that history. Tales of infiltration by the CIA, the KGB, BOSS and British Intelligence might provide the basis of an interesting novel, but they have nothing to do with the cause of the oppressed, and very little relevance to history in general. Nor do I wish to go into the whole sordid business of my own dismissal from Amnesty; that would take another book, the writing of which would not do much for the cause of humanity. I would like to insist at the outset, however, that any criticisms of Amnesty contained in the book – and there are many – are not tainted with any bitter after-taste of the treatment I received. It is true, as I told the British Section's 1981 AGM, that I had experienced more personal animosity from members of Amnesty than I did from members of the South African Security Police, who behaved in a reasonably human fashion, even when they arrived at four o'clock in the morning in search of seditious literature, and that six months of Amnesty harassment had taken a greater toll of me and my family than all the years of South African harassment. I trust that the humanity which rubbed off on to me as a result of my first experience was not completely wiped away by the second.

When writing or speaking about South Africa, I have always pointed out that I am not concerned with the moral turpitude or otherwise of those responsible, but only with what they are doing. I am quite prepared to accept that at least the majority of the members of the South African government, of the security forces, and of the white population as a whole sincerely believe in the rightness of their cause. I am equally willing to extend the same courtesy to those members of Amnesty involved, though not to the extent of gratifying their passion for seeing their names in print. It was their sincerity and dedication which led some to distort the aims of Amnesty, by refusing to accept its inherent limitations, and to claim for it a role which it could not fulfil without positively harming the cause of overcoming oppression; while for some the object of their dedication was simply the organization itself, in which they believed with a touching sincerity. I believed my purpose was to prevent Amnesty from becoming counter-productive, while efficiently pursuing its extremely limited aim. I had no difficulty in doing the latter with respect to all governments; it is easier, I believe, for a committed socialist to do this sincerely than it is for someone from a distinctly right-wing position.

There were some who doubted that I was ever 'committed' to Amnesty and its aim, and they will wish to find those doubts confirmed in this book. Of course I was not committed to Amnesty as an organization any more than I am committed to the Church as an institution; a person cannot be 'entrusted' to or 'put together' with an impersonal entity. I had no desire to enter into any sort of marriage with Amnesty; I prefer the one I have. Nor did I need it as a substitute religion; despite the institutional failings of my present one, I still prefer it. But I would not denigrate the organization's therapeutic value for those who have neither. I did not find an expression of my total political commitment through working for the realization of Amnesty's aims. Indeed, I think it is positively damaging for anybody to do so. My political commitment and, I trust, that of others, is to people and to human needs. Amnesty is concerned with only a part of these needs and a part which, as I shall show, cannot be separated from the whole. One can be, as I was, committed to the part, but not totally and exclusively. A total and exclusive commitment to part of the needs is detrimental to the good of the whole. Even a separate commitment is dangerous, and I think that Amnesty's history shows that, in practice, it is shown to be a danger; the part becomes mistaken for the whole. It is not possible to implant a part of the future ideal society in the present one; it would not work now and it would destroy the wholeness of the future society. That wholeness can be realized partially and progressively, but not bit by bit. That is why, as Miranda says, 'The West abhors few biblical passages as much as it does this: "No one tears a piece from a new cloak to put it on an old cloak; if he does not only will he have torn the new one, but the piece taken from the new will not match the old"' (*Marx and the Bible*, p. 252). In that sense, change must be all or nothing.

The 'part' with which Amnesty deals is the suffering of people but, as I have said, oppression isn't only about suffering. It is the emphasis on this part which leads 'concerned' people to take themselves and what they are doing so seriously and makes them unable even to see the hope and liberation that is present in the suffering. Suffering is obviously not a laughing matter; but puritanical zeal never liberated anyone; neither the zealot nor the victim. The oppressed should teach us to laugh at ourselves and at our puny efforts. If they depended upon us for their liberation, then we would have reason to be serious and even to despair. This does not, of course, provide an excuse for doing nothing, but only a reason for not giving undue importance to any particular action we perform; for not falling into 'the Stalinistic fallacy of one's own achievements'.

The conflict between my two experiences did not arise because of internal

Amnesty politics – the intrigue, the power-seeking and the rest were merely symptoms, just as the different forms of repressive practices are symptoms. The cause was that my understanding of oppression, formed by the experience described, was completely different from one formed in a comfortable middle-class British context. When people in Amnesty spoke of oppression, which they did not very often do, or of human rights, I did not know what they were talking about; and this was not simply because of the Amnesty jargon and love of acronyms. In South Africa I very rarely heard the term 'human rights' used; though the concept was sometimes used as an *ad hominem* argument against those who claimed to believe in them. People were concerned about *being* human, not with *having* rights. In Britain, particularly in Amnesty, the term is bandied around all the time as if everybody knew what it meant. It has become a slogan with very little meaning. Their way of talking about it simply did not relate to my experience of it. I certainly could not recognize the people I knew in 'our prisoners'. 'Our prisoners' were poor helpless creatures for whom one could not help but feel sorry. But feeling sorry for them is a superior, judgemental and entirely inappropriate attitude. It is like 'feeling sorry' for someone who is unemployed, as if the person were to blame for not being in the same fortunate position as you. If you want to feel sorry, you should feel sorry for the people who are to blame (which might include yourself), because they are responsible for the system which causes unemployment or imprisonment. In a sense, those who do not feel sorry for political prisoners because they believe they deserve their fate have a healthier attitude. They simply cannot see, but sometimes I think that 'concerned' people do not actually want to see, because they want to remain happy with what they are doing. I try to give a more charitable explanation and to show that it is the assumptions on which their actions are based which prevent them both from seeing and from doing.

There are many other people in Amnesty, perhaps the vast majority of ordinary members, who do not make any pretentious claims about what they are doing. I would soon have lost any faith at all in Amnesty if I had spent all my time with the activists and ideologues in the London office and had not taken part in meetings organized by members throughout the country. For many of these members their work in Amnesty is only part of a wider political activity, and so they retain a sense of proportion about its importance. If any of them read this book, I trust they will not regard the criticisms as negative, and as destroying the foundation of their work. I would hope that they would rather be led to put more emphasis on their other political work. Some of the most ardent and competent Amnesty workers have already been led to this conclusion by their own experience of the Thatcher government. They have not rejected Amnesty, but they consider it more important to devote their time to their Labour Party work.

For those who believe that the little Amnesty can do is all that can or needs to be done, I can only feel sorry. I am primarily critical of those who believe that Amnesty can do everything; who have made a political ideology out of Amnesty. The ideology, which arises from a false understanding of the problem and therefore of the solution, leads to false value and importance being given to the organization and to the ideologues' position in it. The organization becomes an end in itself and the individual's contribution, not just to Amnesty but to overcoming oppression, is measured in terms of his or her influence and status within the organization. Perhaps that explains why it takes the International Secretariat four months, nine letters and memos, and twenty-one meetings to decide who should represent it at a conference. Some bureaucracy is doubtless needed, but I am sure many would agree with the member who, according to an Amnesty paper, said, 'There is a risk that we are creating a strangely hermetic organization, with more money used for keeping its own structures than for achieving its aims as laid down in the Statute.' The paper denies that this has happened. Yet it must happen to any organization which is concerned only with its *own* understanding of both the problem and the solution, because it is putting itself out of touch with reality. It creates an unreal world of its own, the organization itself necessarily at the centre. It then equates itself with bodies that are 'centres' in the real world, such as governments and, among other things, emulates their bureaucratic structures. Although concern for the organization and even the vying for positions of power within it might well arise from a genuine desire to play a significant part in overcoming oppression, they stem from a false understanding of reality – from an ideology.

This is not a book about Amnesty, it is about the inadequacy of the whole Western approach to human rights. I have used both my own experience of Amnesty and Amnesty publications to illustrate this inadequacy, which is compounded when its political and philosophical origins in liberalism are not even recognized. My experience at Amnesty did complement my South African experience in one respect: the experience of the oppression directly caused by capitalism in South Africa led me to become a committed socialist without, incidentally, having read a word of Marx. The experience at Amnesty further convinced me that neither the depth of the sincerity, nor the intensity of the efforts of those who adhere to the traditional Western liberal ideology – although they haven't even read about it – cannot provide an alternative, nor even be part of the solution.

The criticisms which I make are not negative. They only negate the Western denial of reality and of humanity, which leads to a denial of the hope that is present in the oppressed themselves. While, as I have said, I believe, and will, I trust, demonstrate that the solution can only be found on the basis of our *common* humanity, it is not for us to impose *our* definition of that humanity. We must also listen to, among others, 'Africa's Plea' (quoted by Adam Small in *Drum* and, I presume, one of his own poems):

Africa's Plea

I am not you –
but you will not
give me a chance,
will not let me be 'me'.

'If I were you' –
but you know
I am not you,
yet you will not
let me be 'me'.

You meddle, interfere
in my affairs
as if they were yours
and you were me.

You are unfair, unwise,
foolish to think
that I can be you,
talk, act
and think like you.

God made me 'me'.
He made you 'you'.
For God's sake
Let me be 'me'.

CHAPTER I

WELL-INTENTIONED ARROGANCE

Many people in the West pride themselves both on their respect for human rights in their own countries, and on their concern about the violation of these rights in other countries. In fact, since the signing of the Universal Declaration of Human Rights in 1948 and, more particularly, in the late 1960s and throughout the 1970s, a veritable human rights industry has been spawned. The growth of bureaucratic structures is not necessarily a response to the needs of the oppressed; it often reflects more the needs of the participants, whose self-esteem depends on the size of their desk and the number of telephones on it. What begins as a moral crusade becomes an organization, and the organization becomes an end in itself ready for incorporation into the establishment. Thus Amnesty International, for example, during its crusading days was able to adopt over 900 prisoners with the help of only one full-time and one part-time staff member and on a budget of £10,000; in 1981 the number of prisoners had only increased to 4,000, while the number of staff had risen to 150 and the budget was over £2 million. But it also had its ticker-tape, its computer, its consultative status with the United Nations and its own internal hierarchy within which people vie for power and influence in the organization and hence within the establishment.

All this provides displacement activity and helps people to avoid coming to terms with the reality they claim to be exposing. The protestors of the 1950s, says Jeff Nuttall in *Bomb Culture*, 'developed in their own minds an idealism which acted as an antidote to the sickness attendant on living with the bomb'. Bureaucratic human rights organizations may fulfil a similar function in relation to oppression: the facts are filtered through ideological channels, legalism replaces morality, and reality is kept at a distance so people are able to live with it. In both cases the benefit is 'finally not felt in society but in the practitioners themselves' (ibid., p. 41).

It is true that the moral indignation which gives rise to organizations like Amnesty needs to be harnessed, but it does not need to be submerged. Che

Guevara realized that he ran 'the risk of looking ridiculous' when he said, 'The true revolutionary is led by great feelings of love.' But he said it. An organization, however, does not like to look ridiculous, so it hides behind a legalistic and bureaucratic façade and confines the moral indignation within the limits acceptable to the establishment.

The 'human rights business' took over from the 'sincerity business' of the 1950s as the 'in' thing. As with all multi-national businesses, the headquarters were located in the West and it is the West which has reaped most of the rewards. Just as the West's concern for the 'development' of the Third World in the 1950s served only to increase the poorer countries' economic dependence on the West, so its concern for the rights of oppressed people serves to increase the West's cultural domination. The West has long had a vested interest in oppression; now it seeks to make capital out of its alleged concern for oppressed people. We are all in favour of oppressed people being 'free' – provided it is on our terms. Where there is inequality, either within a nation or between nations,

> the dominant class or nation declares its own values to be *rights*. It does not do this because it is willing to distribute them to others. On the contrary it does this because it possesses these values and also the means of controlling the operative mechanism of justice (which could vindicate the rights of others and ensure their proper distribution). As a result the fight for these values is waged *in an atmosphere where it is doomed to failure from the start*. To believe that the poor nations need merely invoke the shibboleth of human rights is to succumb to a costly naïveté (Segundo, *Evolution and Guilt*, p. 40).

We have defined as fundamental human rights those rights which can be accorded to people in our society without posing any threat to our sociopolitical system. It is we who have decided how societies should be judged and, since our society is taken as the norm, it is not surprising that we measure up to it better than other societies. The West may be worse than other countries in some respects, but we have decided that those respects are not the important ones. The most important aspect, we have decided, is whether a country recognizes human rights as we have defined them. We have decided, for example, that individual freedom is so important that some people must be left free to exploit other people. Inequality, Hayek tells us, is not only the inevitable result of liberty; it is also the justification for it. Those who are on the receiving end of inequality, which is the vast majority of the world's population, might well take a different view. The fact that there are over three million unemployed people in Britain might be a greater condemnation of our system than the imprisoning of people in a 'developing' country. And is our treatment of mentally ill people any less evil than the Soviet Union's abuse of psychiatry to control and punish political prisoners? In both cases the reason for the treatment is that people do not conform to the norms of society; the only difference is that our norms are social rather than political. A Soviet dissident may be just as mad, according to the norms of his society, as many of the people locked up in our mental institutions are, according to ours. Unlike totalitarian states, we can tolerate the views of political deviants, but there is no place in our competitive, consumerist, status-ridden society for social deviants. We have decided, therefore, that it is more important to be concerned about political deviants in other countries. Our own deviants we classify as mad or as common criminals. A person in the West who objects to the private owner-ship of property and relieves somebody of it is guilty of a crime, whereas a person in the Soviet Union who objects to collectivism is making a political protest. It is less threatening and more rewarding to be concerned about the problems of other countries than those of our own and of our responsibility for all of them.

A black South African friend of mine tells the story of his visit to an anti-apartheid organization (not the Anti-Apartheid Movement) in the United States. With great pride, they showed him all the posters, badges, leaflets and books that they had produced and asked for his opinion. He replied, 'I only hope that the Blacks in South Africa do not succeed in overthrowing the nationalist government.' 'Why?' they asked. 'Because you would all be out of a job,' he said. There might be a hint of cynicism in that view. On the other hand, one cannot doubt the sincerity and dedication of the people concerned. Admirable as these qualities are, however, they do not necessarily safeguard people from the pitfalls to which Western arrogance and assumed cultural superiority are prone.

When I was in South Africa, and had been given the government-accorded hallmark of political respectability by being banned and house-arrested, I was automatically on the list of people whom visiting dignitaries and human rights luminaries had to see. I eventually found myself *defending* the policies of the South African government against such people, because of their simplistic understanding of the problems and their patronizing attitude about the ability of the people to do anything for themselves. Many of them, even if they were prepared to give vast amounts of financial aid, were part of the problem, not of the solution. They seemed to believe that the Afrikaner nationalist was a different species from his capitalist counterpart in Europe, and that his sole purpose in life was to persecute Blacks; whereas, in fact, his purpose was essentially the same as theirs. Others acknowledged that the nationalists were much the same as any other capitalist and thought they would desist from their excesses if only one could enter into a dialogue with them and persuade them to 'play the game'. The Blacks, on the other hand, needed only a little Western enlightenment, encouragement and organization. No one could have had more simplistic ideas than Jimmy Carter's ambassador for human rights, Andrew Young, who seemed to think that if only enough Blacks could be persuaded to march down the main street of Johannesburg singing 'We Shall Overcome', all problems would be solved.

The 'human rights industry' is a particularly productive field for bureaucrats and academics, especially if they are fond of overseas travel. A. H. Robertson opens his book *Human Rights in the World* with the statement: 'The number of Declarations, Conventions and Covenants adopted and the number of new organs – committees, commissions and courts – already created or shortly to be established are such as to provide extensive material for study and research for the lawyer and the political scientist.' Doubtless they are; but it is doubtful whether they achieve much more. It is considered essential for such research to go and see oppression at work, and scholarships are always available for this purpose, but it is little consolation to oppressed people to know that they are providing the raw material for a Ph.D. thesis. After all the stories I have heard of Africans deliberately misleading prying researchers, such as anthropologists inquiring into their sexual habits or religious customs, I have little faith in such research.

We cannot assume that oppressed people necessarily and blindly welcome any display of interest and concern about their plight by people in the West. Perhaps some of them do; but we cannot *assume* that they all do. Human rights organizations are quick to rebut the argument that their activities are an unjustifiable intervention in the affairs of another state. But they do not consider whether such activities are an unjustifiable intervention in the affairs of the people about whom they are concerned. Amnesty International, for example, does not consult the prisoners about whether they want to be adopted, or whether they have any objections to 'courteously worded letters' being sent on their behalf to their political enemies. It assumes that if a person is in prison the most important consideration is to get him or her out, regardless of any wider political implications. There are, however, many people (particularly political leaders) in prison, who believe that their staying is more important for the good of their people than their own release would be – whether this release was on condition that they left the country, or simply a propaganda exercise for the government. They do not distinguish between their own individual good and the good of the people. Nevertheless, there are well-intentioned Amnesty people who would do their utmost to get them out, believing that their individual right not to be imprisoned is more important than the political good of the people. (Such enthusiasts could have had a field-day in obtaining releases during the Anti-Pass Law Campaign in South Africa at the time of Sharpeville. Thousands of people refused to pay fines or even to apply for bail because they wanted to make a political point by staying in prison. The government would have been only too glad to accommodate appeals for their release.) Likewise, the demands that Amnesty makes on governments, such as legislation to ensure the proper conduct of trials or even the release of prisoners of conscience, might well not reflect the priorities of the people. One is hardly likely to discover these priorities by talking, as Amnesty does, to the people responsible for the oppression. It is quite possible that a government could meet such demands and yet reinforce its domination of the people. Amnesty is more easily satisfied than the people; but surely the object of the exercise is not self-satisfaction.

Even if prisoners were released without the conditions which gave rise to their opposition being changed, their 'freedom' would be shortlived, since most of them would presumably resume the activity in which they had previously been engaged; African National Congress activists, for example, do so even after having spent up to fifteen years on Robben Island. If they were prepared not to do that, the government would not be particularly concerned about keeping them in prison; even the most oppressive governments do not imprison people for purely punitive reasons. The purpose of the South African Internal Security Act, for example, is preventative; it allows for the detention of anyone whom a police officer might suspect of thinking about doing something subversive!

Neither arresting nor seeking the release of prisoners is an end in itself. Mr Jimmy Kruger, the South African Minister of Justice who was 'left cold' by Steve Biko's death, once assured all banned and house-arrested people that he regularly reviewed their restriction orders and that he was quite prepared to release anybody once he was convinced, on the basis of reports from the Security Police, that their 'mental attitude' had changed. This prompted my wife to write an open letter to him, saying that she sincerely hoped that I would not be released since she was sure (though she could not quote me) that I had not, and would not want anybody to think I had, changed my 'mental attitude'; and, in any case, she did not consider my own two special security policemen to be competent to make such a judgement. When I was released, which was at the time when Vorster was making 'concessions' to give some credibility to his policy of détente, I suggested that it was due to Kruger wishing to make his contribution to this cosmetic exercise by adding a touch of underarm deodorant.

The fact that I had not wanted to be released in such circumstances and that I was sure that there were thousands of others in the same position caused great consternation among Amnesty members, who saw this as a denial of the *raison d'être* of the organization. But that is already denied by Amnesty's own rule that members, in their work for prisoners, must never break the law of the country in which they live; which implies that either the law or the organization is more important than people's consciences. If that advice were followed by everybody, there would be no prisoners of conscience on whose behalf Amnesty could work. An inbred respect for law and the assumption of the supreme importance of individual liberty make it very difficult for people to understand and to support those who share neither of these concerns. A very dedicated and experienced Amnesty worker once told me, for example, of a 'case' on which his group had worked: after, though not necessarily because of, a great deal of effort on their part the prisoner was released; he immediately resumed his political activity and was promptly arrested again; the group renewed its efforts on his behalf, and he was later released into exile; after some time in exile he returned to take up his activities once more, and again he was arrested. The group considered they were justified in thinking that 'he had asked for it', and only with reluctance took up their pens again.

Anybody who opposes a repressive regime is asking for trouble; if the main concern of such people was to avoid trouble for themselves, there would be no prisoners and also no prospect of change. Fortunately, however, there are many people who are prepared to go on asking for trouble until they gain their freedom, not their individual liberty. They do not, therefore, necessarily welcome intervention, however well intentioned it might be, which is foreign not only geographically but also ideologically.

Sincerity and good intentions are no substitute for a sound political judgement. And it is the oppressed people themselves who are in the best position to make political judgements about their condition. This judgement is not necessarily dulled by years of imprisonment. Even after eighteen years in prison, Nelson Mandela's judgement was sharp enough to know that he would not be furthering the cause of his people by consorting with US congressmen, however sincere and well meaning they were. Nor was he concerned that this, for once, put him on the same side as the South African government. The government refused the congressmen's request to see him, but his wife and lawyer were quick to point out that, even if the government had agreed, Mandela would have refused.

It is patronizing to expect prisoners to be grateful to anyone who deigns to speak to them; it is the grossest arrogance to assume that they want anyone to speak *for* them. Amnesty International, however, has always seen the sending of 'missions' as one of its most effective methods. Originally one or two members of a group sometimes went to intercede with a government about 'their' prisoner and there was probably little harm in that. There might also be something to be said for the sort of 'back-door diplomacy' engaged in by Sean MacBride when he went to appeal to the Czech government on behalf of Archbishop Beran (the Archbishop himself was convinced that it helped). But the present practice of sending 'high-level' missions is a different matter and is a typical example of the arrogant Western assumption that they know best. If the people of any country wanted such an intervention they could ask for it either directly or through their exile organizations. Amnesty, however, appears to be more concerned about its own views and those of the governments. Missions are sent either at the request of a government (for what purpose other than to have an opportunity of whitewashing their regime?), or on Amnesty's own initiative. But 'in all cases the government is informed of the mission', and great care is taken not to embarrass them: 'the Rules require that they [the delegates] make no public statements before, after or during a mission'. There are also 'careful procedures and practices not only to ensure that AI business is conducted effectively but also to minimize any risk of potential damage to AI's work, its credibility or [at last!] the interests of prisoners and others where the mission is taking place: care in the selection of delegates [a title helps], careful arrangements with the government concerned, thorough and professional briefing of the delegates, strict adherence to the rules for delegates' conduct and other means'. There is no indication that these 'other means' include any consultation with the people or their true representatives. The purpose of such missions is to conduct business 'relevant to AI concerns'. But the violation of human rights is not Amnesty's concern: it is everybody's concern. Above all it is the concern of the victims, who are neither witless nor helpless.

The more formal and high-powered such missions are (whether they are sent by Amnesty or anybody else), the graver the danger that they will be of more value to the oppressive government than to the oppressed people. Some people might actually rather stay in prison than have such recognition and respect accorded to the government which they oppose. I doubt whether British Leyland workers, for example, would be grateful to a group of foreign well-wishers who decided to take it upon themselves to try to reach a settlement on their behalf over a cup of tea with Mrs Thatcher. Why should oppressed people in other countries feel differently?

In the light of the West's history of war, oppression and exploitation at home and abroad, it is difficult to see how we can feel competent to offer advice to anybody. Yet we still insist on doing so. The 'Big Powers' even seek to make a virtue out of their efforts to determine the future shape of Namibia for example – efforts which are guaranteed simply to exchange one form of domination for another. Even lesser powers, such as the churches, arrogate to themselves the moral right to insist that the Constitution includes such measures as guarantees for the protection of minority groups. But there is nothing 'moral' about these measures; they are Western. They have not been particularly effective in the West and there are no grounds for assuming they would be in Africa. Nor are they necessarily desirable. Steve Biko, for one, certainly did not believe they were,

> because guaranteeing minority rights implies the recognition of portions of the community on a race basis. We believe that in our country there shall be no minority, there shall be no majority, just the people. And those people will have the same status before the law and they will have the same political rights before the law. So in a sense it will be a completely non-racial egalitarian society (Stubbs (ed.), Steve Biko, *I Write What I Like*, p. 149).

But at the level of inter-governmental and non-governmental organizations, of churches, and even of individuals, the West knows best. Everything must be done our way.

There are of course people, including human rights activists, who criticize the West, both for its appalling record in relation to human rights and for its present practices. The criticism, however, is aimed at showing that Western countries are as bad as the Soviet Union, Chile or South Africa in their suppression of individual liberty and in their treatment of dissidents. Comparisons are made, for example, between the number of people who die in police custody in Britain and South Africa or between the powers of the Home Secretary and the Soviet Politburo; attention is drawn to the lack of freedom of information, to restrictions on trade union activities and to the powers of the police. On these and many similar criteria the West does not come out very well. It is true, for example, that a South African Minister of Justice once said that he would willingly exchange the powers given to him by the whole panoply of South African security laws for the special powers given to the authorities in Northern Ireland. But to argue on those terms is to accept the norms of the Western ruling classes. The degree of oppressiveness among governments cannot be judged on the basis of who throws more people into jail, who tortures them more brutally, or who executes them more summarily. The worse other countries can be shown to be in these respects, the better the defenders of the status quo in the West feel because, they can argue, although we may not be perfect, at least we are not as bad as that. We may concede that Western countries are not as bad *in that way*; but this does not mean that they are not as bad. Given the same historical, economic, social and political conditions as in these other countries, there is no reason, as we shall see later, for believing that Western governments would not act in the same brutal fashion. They do not do so now only because they do not need to. The West has taken to heart, and applied to society, Rousseau's advice to teachers:

Let [the child] believe that he is always in control, though it is always you who really controls. There is no subjugation so perfect as that which keeps the appearance of freedom, for in that way one captures volition itself. The poor baby, knowing nothing, able to do nothing, having learned nothing, is he not at your mercy? Can you not arrange everything in the world which surrounds him? Can you not influence him as you wish? His work, his play, his pleasures, his pains, are not all these in your hands and without his knowing? Doubtless he ought only to do what he wants; but he ought to want to do only what you want him to do; he ought not to take a step which you have not forseen; he ought not to open his mouth without your knowing what he will say (*Émile*).

The West is at least as bad (in fact I shall argue it is essentially the same) as the oppressive regimes, not only because of its historical responsibility for the conditions in many repressive countries (the United States is responsible for Chile, El Salvador and Latin America in general, and Europe for Africa and much of Asia) but also because of its present collusion with such regimes. If the West is prepared to have trade and other relations with, and particularly if it is willing to sell arms to oppressive governments, then it shares the responsibility for what those governments are doing to their own people, whatever it might say to the contrary. It is prepared to do this because it shares the oppressors' belief in the fundamental principle that political and economic interests are more important than people.

This was clearly evidenced in the British Labour government's handling of the Rhodesian Unilateral Declaration of Independence. An effective oil boycott could have brought down the Smith regime and thus averted a long-drawn-out war, during which thousands of people were killed, and the continuance of a regime which imprisoned, tortured or killed thousands of others and which uprooted hundreds of thousands of people from their homes. An unequivocal commitment to sanctions, however, would have entailed a threat to British trade and other economic links with South Africa. So the commitment was never made.

Martin Bailey, who first exposed the extent of the oil sanctions busting and the British government's connivance with it and with the subsequent cover-up, concludes his study of the whole 'Oilgate' scandal by saying:

> There is no neat explanation for Oilgate; no individual oil executive, civil servant or politician can be singled out as the villain of the story. Oilgate is more disturbing. It is an indictment of a political system that allows a major aspect of the most important foreign policy issue which Britain has faced in recent years to be treated as a mockery – behind closed doors. But is Oilgate a story in which everything went wrong? Or is it just a more dramatic and well-documented example of the political process in Britain today?

An even greater indictment of the political system than the secrecy which surrounds its workings is the fact that it is designed to protect the interests of the powerful and to put economic concerns before people; particularly if they are black and live – or die – five thousand miles away.

President Jimmy Carter's simplistic, moralistic approach to the question of human rights did little to improve either the image or the practice of the West. There is no doubt that he had a genuine moral concern, based on his religious beliefs, but it is also true that after Nixon any sign of moral probity was a vote-catcher. Further, in the aftermath of the Vietnam war, American public opinion was prepared for some handwashing; for which there was plenty of scope. A study had shown, for example, that there was 'a strong positive correlation between the amount of US bilateral aid to Latin American countries and the propensity of those governments to torture their own citizens' (Kommers and Loescher (eds.), *Human Rights and American Foreign Policy*, p. 182). Often US involvement has been even more direct: the US Army School of the Americas, in the Panama Canal Zone, was reported to have trained over 30,000 Latin American military officers between 1949 and 1976; assistance in the form of training or supplies had been given to over one million foreign policemen; 'technology transfers' had been made to some of the most brutal secret police services in the world – the DINA in Chile, SAVAK in Iran, BOSS in South Africa, and the Korean CIA; backing had been given to right-wing forces in the Congo, Angola, Guyana, Indo-China, the Dominican Republic,

El Salvador – in fact anywhere where there was a 'communist threat' to US political and economic interests.

Carter wished to be 'free of that inordinate fear of communism which once led us to embrace any dictator who joined us in that fear' (Commencement Address, May 1977). His policy did prevent the granting of loans and the sale of arms to some repressive regimes, but he hardly lived up to the promise given in his inaugural address that 'our commitment to human rights must be absolute'. As Warren Christopher pointed out, 'When the human rights performance of the recipient [of security assistance] is unsatisfactory, we may continue to provide aid because of our overriding national security interests, but not without expressing concern' (Kommers and Loescher, op. cit., p. 214).

There is not much point in having a policy which 'is rooted in our moral values, which never change', if one of those moral values is the overriding importance of American interests. It means only that one should be concerned about human rights, provided it does not cost too much. With such a presupposition, the policy must run 'the risk of dividing the world into two categories: countries unimportant enough to be hectored about human rights and countries important enough to get away with murder' (R. J. Barnet, quoted in Kommers and Loescher, p. 224).

'America is a poor second to Russia when it comes to choice of an ally,' said Steve Biko, 'in spite of Black opposition to any form of domination by a foreign power. Heavy investment in the South African economy, bilateral trade with South Africa, cultural exchanges in the fields of sport and music and, of late, joint political ventures like the Vorster–Kissinger exercise are amongst the sins with which America is accused' (Stubbs (ed.), Steve Biko, I Write What I Like, p. 140). America cannot absolve itself of these sins either by expressions of concern or by seeking to impose its moral values. Human rights, as Carter understood them, did not even feature among the 'minimum requirements' which Biko laid down for an acceptable American foreign policy in relation to South Africa.

Carter said, and doubtless believed, that his policy was 'designed to serve mankind'. But it was not possible for it to achieve this end because, as he also said, the policy was 'reinforced by our material wealth and by our military power'. It is the way America has accumulated its wealth and the way it has used its military power – it has intervened militarily in other countries' affairs 150 times in the past two hundred years – which have caused and which perpetuate much of the suffering of mankind.

I make no apology for being so negative about the role of the West – of which I too am part – in respect of human rights and I will return to the theme. I actually believe in the power of negative thinking when it is opposed to a positive thinking which, in order to make people feel good, deludes them into believing that they are achieving great things when in fact they are reinforcing evil. There is no virtue in positive thinking which leads people to accept the myths of which Paulo Freire speaks: the myth of their own superiority; the myth that they 'save the poor'; the myth of the absolute ignorance of the oppressed. We need the oppressed more than they need us. We need them not as objects of exploitation for our material benefit, nor as objects of charity for our spiritual benefit. We need them because it is only they who can challenge us and change us. As Frantz Fanon says:

> To educate the masses politically means ... to try relentlessly and passionately to teach the masses that everything depends on them; that if we stagnate it is their responsibility, and that if we go forward it is due to them too, that there is no such thing as a demiurge, that there is no famous man who will take the responsibility for everything, but that the demiurge is the people themselves and that the magic hands are finally only the hands of the people (*The Wretched of the Earth*, pp. 157–8).

I am not suggesting that we should simply wallow masochistically in our guilt. We cannot, however, rid ourselves of this guilt either by professing that we have the right *ideas* about justice and freedom and are prepared to make the right sort of noises about their denial, or by expressing our sympathy for the victims. But before we can do anything we need to be aware of our guilt:

> The philosophy of oppression, perfected and refined through civilizations as a true culture of injustice, does not achieve its greatest triumph when its propagandists knowingly inculcate it; rather the triumph is achieved when this philosophy has become so deeply rooted in the spirits of the oppressors themselves and their ideologues that they are not even aware of their guilt (Miranda, *Marx and the Bible*, p. xi).

That is probably even more true of Western oppressors than it is of Second or Third World ones, who are relative newcomers to the practice of oppression. Like the well-known homosexual, the West is not practising, it is an expert.

We in the West assume that we have all the answers and that the world would be set to rights if people only listened to, and followed us. We do not appear to have learned from our history. A lot of people, however, are, by their rejection of Western influences, telling us we are wrong. We will never hear them if we continue to shout out our 'answers' louder and louder. Becoming more knowledgeable about the facts of violations of human rights and increasing the volume of our protest about them neither creates an awareness of oppression nor helps with finding solutions. Knowledge of the facts as something entirely removed from ourselves can be positively harmful if it is used to make scapegoats and to bolster our complacency. Inundating people with information about more and more horrendous examples of the violation of human rights will be counter-productive unless it challenges that complacency and makes people aware of their responsibility for, and involvement with, the history of oppression. Such an awareness of oppression should make us prepared to listen to what people are saying by their words and actions. We should not only be prepared to defend people's right to freedom of expression even though they are wrong and we do not agree with them; we should also be willing to consider that they might actually be right, and that we are wrong and have been for a very long time. We might, however, find what they are saying rather uncongenial. We prefer, therefore, to ask governments to open their prisons – to treat people in the same way as we do – rather than to demand that they open their ears, since we do not do that either. This is as applicable to Britain as to any other country. British society cannot conceive of 'law and order' as being oppressive, so they cannot believe that the youth of Brixton and Toxteth might be saying something worthwhile to them by rioting.

It might be argued, in defence of the Western system, that at least I am free to say such things, whereas in South Africa, for example, I would be silenced. But all that proves is that it is not necessary to silence people in Britain, because social controls are such that there is no danger of anybody actually doing anything about what anyone says. Once people begin to do so we will see how much difference there is between British and any other rulers. Even the South African government is prepared to be tolerant of the expression of views, provided they are sure that Blacks will take no notice of them. The most radical articles on revolutionary Marxism are allowed to be published because they are couched in such abstruse, academic language that black workers and peasants are not likely to be moved to action by them.

I am not falling into the trap of using the same argument as the defenders of the status quo and saying that, since the West is so bad, other countries are not as bad as they are usually judged to be and so there is less need for us to be concerned. Firstly, I am saying that we have no call to be self-righteous in our condemnations or arrogant in our proposed solutions.

Secondly, I question whether anyone who, either consciously or un-consciously, assumes the values and standards of Western society can make any contribution to the struggle against oppression, wherever it occurs. A further more disturbing feature of the 'Oilgate' scandal was that there was, as Anthony Sampson says in his introduction to Bailey's book, 'plenty of evidence that the British voters, together with much of the Press, were quite happy to be deceived (by government ministers) in order not to be faced with a painful decision'. The decision being whether their own material interests were more important than the lives of (mainly black) Rhodesians. Given a clear choice, there are doubtless many people who would be prepared to make some sacrifice. The choice, however, is not usually made clear, and even the most well-intentioned people in their sincerest expressions of concern for oppressed people are inhibited by their implicit acceptance of Western norms and by their involvement with Western interests.

While I was under house-arrest I was given permission to come to England to visit my father who was very ill. As a real, live prisoner of conscience from the country that everyone loves to hate, I had easy access to any of the great and the good who could be considered even remotely progressive. I made use of this opportunity to have discussions with MPs, lords, newspaper editors and other eminent people. One evening when I was setting off to meet a particularly distinguished journalist, my father, a man of great native intelligence but little formal education and an ardent trade unionist and Labour Party member, said, 'Why do you spend your time with these people? They are not our people and they are not going to help the people you are concerned about. You should be talking to ordinary trade unionists.' I explained that these were the people who formed public opinion; they were the people with power and influence and so we needed their help. I was, however, completely wrong and he was right. Such people will doubtless express their concern, but they will not do anything to bring about real change. They will not because the nearer they are to the centres of power the less it is in their interest to do so.

If those responsible for the more subtle forms of oppression in the West share the same fundamental principles as those responsible for the more brutal forms of oppression in other countries, and if the former are prepared at least to connive at the activities of the latter, the closer one is allied to the former the less one will or can do about the latter. Those responsible in both cases are not just the politicians, but also big business, the judiciary, the media and, sometimes, the Church and others. To assume that such people can do anything is to imply that the different forms of oppression in the West and in other countries are totally unrelated, and to believe that

Western domination of the world ceased with the end of colonialism. In any event, 'Mind in all its manifestations is never only what it is, but also what it was . . .' (quoted in Freire, *Cultural Action for Freedom*, p. 21). We cannot simply shake off our history of oppression.

This is a lesson which has certainly not been learnt by human rights organizations. Instead, their approach is based on the belief that the more important a person is the more significant his or her support for the cause is. But, as the Latin American theologian Rubem Alves says, 'only the oppressed have the will to abolish the power presuppositions which are at the root of their oppression' (*Tomorrow's Child*, p. 199). Others might be moved to protest about the more naked expressions of these presuppositions, but they have neither the ability nor the desire to abolish them. It is the people who have least to lose in our own society, who also have the least to lose from change in countries which are dominated, or at least supported by us. These are the people, therefore, who are most likely to be willing and able to be of help to their fellow oppressed. The ruling classes, however, have a common interest in preventing oppressed people from realizing their common cause. An elitist approach to the question of oppression, therefore, is welcomed by the ruling classes both in the West and in other oppressive countries. In the West, because it obviates the danger of the oppressed there becoming even more aware of their oppression; in other countries, because they know it will be ineffective, since it will not address itself to the real problem.

Cultivating an elitist approach, as many human rights activists do, is playing into the hands of the oppressors. When Amnesty, for example, says that in seeking members it should 'focus on quality rather than quantity', one wonders who is to define 'quality'. One suspects that power, influence and privilege in our society will be its main components. The participation of lawyers, doctors, businessmen and politicians is already valued more than that of ordinary people with no letters after their names. Apart from any other considerations, surely these are the very people who governments, particularly socialist ones, would expect to have nothing better to do than to write letters of protest. If working-class people had taken the trouble to write, then they might be impressed. The present trend within Amnesty to distance itself from the trade union movement is further evidence of a failure to understand the indivisibility of oppression, and of a desire to remain respectable in the eyes of the establishment. It is also symptomatic of the way in which the internal politics of the various national sections of Amnesty reflect not only general Western assumptions but also the specific politics of their particular country. This trend started in the United States during the Reagan administration and in Britain under Thatcher. But it is not possible to remain pure in the eyes of such representatives of the establishment and still to be concerned about the cause of the oppressed.

It is only fair to say, however, that Amnesty does not officially claim to be dealing with oppression; it deals with the persecution of individuals. It is possible that its limited aim can be best achieved through a dialogue between elites in the West and elites in other oppressive countries: after all, the people about whom Amnesty is primarily concerned tend themselves to be part of the elite (not that that is any justification for their being persecuted); only 25 per cent of adopted prisoners of conscience are peasants, workers, or trade unionists. Amnesty has in the past recognized this. Its 1975 Report on Torture acknowledges that

> in most of the world only the famous or the wealthy are likely to be able to focus international attention on their plight once they are imprisoned and ill-treated. Only the educated – and specifically the European educated – are likely to know that an organization such as Amnesty International exists and wishes to alleviate their situation ... The incarceration of government ministers, of poets and musicians, of internationally respected professors or physicians will be noticed by others than their families. Approaches will be made on their behalf to the Press, to international organizations, to Amnesty International ... But what of the student, the taxi driver, the worker or the farmer?

All that is asked on behalf of the other victims of oppression is that they be treated humanely. But it cannot extend that aim and yet exclude the very people who could best help to achieve it. I believe, as I shall explain in the next chapter, that there is a place for human rights Red Cross work. It can, and does, prevent a tremendous amount of human suffering; and it can be done impartially and apolitically. Such work cannot, however, free people from oppression, nor even defend their human rights any more than the Red Cross, for all its good work, can put an end to war. Nobody blames the Red Cross for that and I am not blaming Amnesty for not doing something that it was not intended, and is not equipped to do.

In its early years Amnesty seemed positively to encourage a comparison between its own role and that of the International Red Cross. As an early publication said: 'Provided it [Amnesty] sticks closely to its limited and practicable objectives, it can become a permanent influence on world opinion and an institution which ultimately does as much useful work to reduce suffering as the Red Cross.' Nowadays this comparison is seen by many within Amnesty as being a slight on the importance of its work.

That in turn, of course, is a slight on the Red Cross. But the relief of human suffering is an eminently worthwhile aim. It is, moreover, the only aim that Amnesty can pursue in an impartial and apolitical way. Whatever forms oppression and the resistance to it take, there will always be casualties. Amnesty can only try to ensure that these be as few as possible and that even these be treated in a humane way. 'Amnesty is in essence a humanitarian movement; its underlying purpose is to reduce human suffering ... [it] aims to bring home to people the amount of needless suffering caused by coercion of opinion.' Millions of people are struggling to free themselves from oppression and people are needed to care for the casualties. But people are also needed to join in the struggle; to take sides. The struggle is primarily the task of the oppressed people themselves and, secondarily, of those who are willing to give them political support in a consciously partisan way.

It is surely better, however, for people who wish to remain politically unsullied – or who do not wish to have their own political assumptions challenged – to be engaged as human rights stretcher-bearers whenever they are needed, than for them simply to spend their time condemning the Soviet Union and making excuses for right-wing governments. Their efforts only become counter-productive when it is claimed that they are thus combating oppression and fighting for human rights, or if they distract attention from the need for direct political action.

Amnesty was not intended to be either an alternative to other human rights organizations which were concerned with particular countries and ideologies, or an amalgamation of their interests. It was based rather on the highest common factor between such groups and other individuals; its aim was to agree on the minimum that *everybody* could expect *all* governments to do with respect to freedom of expression – namely, that they should be tolerant. Its appeal was to the apathetic rather than to the activist: 'Our main adversary is the apathy of free people who either cannot be bothered to register disapproval or who have no effective means of doing so' (*Amnesty*, vol. I). It was not in any way meant to undermine the efforts of those who wished to make greater demands on oppressive governments. Such people tended to be on the left of the political spectrum; consequently, all human rights activity, unless it was avowedly anti-Soviet, was, and possibly still is seen as a left-wing preoccupation. Benenson wanted to show that there was at least a small area of concern to which people of a more conservative disposition could devote their energies. Left-wing activists could be expected to take Amnesty's concern on board in addition to their own, but they could be joined by others who wanted to travel only a little of the way.

With regard to the work done for prisoners: to Benenson's mind, its effect on the people *doing* it was just as important as its effect on the prisoners themselves. 'Anyone who in any way, however slight, becomes concerned in their suffering,' he said, 'does himself some good' (ibid., p. 16, para. 61). More support might have been forthcoming from left-wing people had they been asked only to work for prisoners in right-wing countries; on the other hand, governments might have been expected to respond more readily to appeals from people who shared their political views. Neither of these approaches, however, would have done anything for the education of Amnesty members themselves in the practice of tolerance or in the need for dialogue, which is what Benenson was concerned with. He hoped that such education would lead people to question their own and their society's values, and to take up broader issues beyond the immediate concerns of Amnesty.

What has happened with Amnesty, and with other organizations, is that they have confused the right to freedom of opinion with human rights, and confused the violation of individual rights with oppression; even more important, they have accepted the Western individualist view of man and society as being the only view. They therefore believe that in defending the right to freedom of opinion they are defending human rights and over-coming oppression. Nevertheless, something can still be achieved apoliti-cally: Amnesty has succeeded in this, and can continue to do so if it will only cease trying to outdo the United Nations in bureaucracy and if it recognizes its limitations despite, or perhaps because of, the 'quality' of the support it seeks. I am not concerned so much with making a critique of Amnesty as with using it as an example of both the potential and the limitations of an apolitical approach to human rights.

CHAPTER 2

AMNESTY INTERNATIONAL
AND HUMAN RIGHTS

'Human rights,' says Amnesty's Chairperson, José Zalaquett, 'transcend the boundaries of nation, race and belief.' If they do, they also transcend people. 'Human rights' is an abstraction; rights take on meaning only when they are realized in a person in a particular time and place. There are no human rights which can be claimed as absolute; consequently, there are none which can be defended apolitically, since political considerations are among the factors which relativize them. The most we can say is that people have the right not to be subjected to arbitrary control over their thoughts and actions, and the right not to be treated in a less than human fashion. These are not, strictly speaking, absolutes, since both 'arbitrary' and 'human' are relative terms; not everybody in every time and place would agree on their interpretation. One cannot infer, as Zalaquett does, that there must be 'some universally accepted values' because 'an organization embracing the human rights activism of thousands of members throughout the world' needs them! (That is rather like Eisenhower's statement: 'Our government makes no sense, unless it is founded in a deeply felt religious faith – and I don't care what it is!')

Amnesty was originally concerned not with human rights as such, nor even with the right to individual liberty, but simply with freedom of opinion and freedom of religion. Further, it was not concerned with the nature of these freedoms as rights; it certainly did not consider them to be absolute rights. As Benenson wrote in his book, which was part of the launching of the original 'Appeal for Amnesty',

> Let us all recognize that there are situations when the security of the state is threatened, in which the government feel obliged to arrest their opponents. But there has been of late too little willingness to release them once the emergency is over. Again we can understand that there are situations, particularly in newly emerged states, where it is difficult to govern in the face of sustained criticism. But this fact alone does not entitle a government to keep its critics *permanently* imprisoned.

As an alternative, he suggested, 'when the political and economic situation of a country does not permit unbridled criticism, then a government should offer to its most vociferous critics the opportunity to seek asylum abroad' (p. 13).

What Benenson was concerned with, therefore, was a plea for tolerance, not a demand for rights. Moreover, it was simply a plea for the tolerance of *ideas*. The first formal statement of Amnesty's aims makes this clear:

> The Amnesty movement is composed of peoples of all nationalities, politics, religious and social views, who are determined to work together in defence of *freedom of the mind* ...
>
> The principal object of Amnesty is to mobilize public opinion in defence of those men and women who are imprisoned because their *ideas* are unacceptable to their governments. It has been formed so that there should be some central, international organization capable of concentrating efforts to secure the release of these 'Prisoners of Conscience', and to secure world-wide recognition of Articles 18–19 of the Universal Declaration of Human Rights. Essentially an impartial organization as regards religion and politics, it aims at uniting groups in different countries working towards the same end – the freedom and dignity of the *human mind* (my italics).

The articles of the Universal Declaration referred to mention only freedom of practice with respect to religion or belief. As to freedom of opinion and expression, Article 19 states only that 'this right includes freedom to hold opinions without interference and to seek, receive and impart information and ideas through any media and regardless of frontiers'. A publication by the British Section of Amnesty in 1964 leaves no doubt about Amnesty's very restricted understanding of freedom of opinion. It stresses that the definition of a 'prisoner of conscience' – that is, one for whose release Amnesty would work – 'excludes those who *take action* to implement their ideas, just as much as it excludes those who advocate violence. Some people are disappointed by this narrow definition, arguing that, if a man feels strongly enough about his opinions, he ought to be allowed to put them into action. This may be so, but a great many people who believe passionately in freedom of opinion would reject that proposition. Amnesty exists to bring together *all* people who believe in human freedom and it must therefore have as its foundation a proposition which is universally agreed. This is not to say that those who want to should not support the cause of imprisoned men of action. There are many nationalist, political and religious organizations concerned with the defence of men of action. But Amnesty is concerned *only with the defence of opinions.*'

Benenson was inspired to launch his 'Appeal for Amnesty' when he read of two friends being arrested and imprisoned on a charge of treason simply for making a critical remark about the government while dining in a restaurant in Portugal. Such were the people whose views, Benenson thought, should be tolerated; and he considered that even the most oppressive government might be persuaded by the pressure of public opinion to do that much. He was well aware that much more needed to be done; but he was also aware that no more *could* be done from an apolitical standpoint. I would not argue that an organization should not develop and, if necessary, modify and re-interpret its aims in the light of changing circumstances and of its own experience. If, however, Amnesty were to modify its original understanding of 'freedom of opinion', and if it were to move from pleading for tolerance to demanding rights, it would also have to modify, indeed abandon, its claim to being apolitical. This would destroy its whole *raison d'être*, which is to involve people who do not want to be political.

If its aims are extended, political judgements are necessarily made; and if these are not made consciously and deliberately, it is almost inevitable that they will reflect the politics of the status quo. One cannot avoid making political judgements by claiming that the right to freedom of opinion is absolute and that the right of the individual always takes precedence over that of the state. Both this claim (a claim made by Amnesty) and its direct opposite are made from a political position. Thus Thomas Hammarberg, the former Chairman and present Secretary General, wrote in the 1978 Annual Report: 'Basic human rights must stand above *all* other political ambitions and should be respected under *all* circumstances and in *all* situations' (my italics). Any position on the relationship between the rights of the individual and the rights of the state is a political one, and I cannot find a more extreme expression of liberal individualism than Hammarberg's. As we shall see in the next chapter, it is not based on the generally accepted liberal philosophical tradition, nor is it endorsed by the United Nations' documents.

Even Amnesty admits that the rights of any individual are limited by the rights of others. But one individual cannot be free to decide what the rights of other individuals are or when they are being infringed. Some restriction on the rights of some individuals is therefore necessary in order to safeguard the rights of other individuals. The task of government is to restrict the liberty of all as little as possible in order to protect the liberty of all as much as possible. One cannot, therefore, assume that any restriction imposed by a government on an individual is wrong. The 'basic human rights' with which Amnesty is concerned are freedom of expression, association, assembly or movement. These, it claims, must never be restricted.

A government is not concerned with the abstract truth or falsity of a person's views, nor with whether their other actions are 'objectively' right or wrong. The government and, generally speaking, the people involved are concerned about the political and social effects of the exercise of these rights. The government is, or at least claims to be, concerned with whether or not this is harmful to the common good, that is to other people and their rights. It cannot be argued that whatever the effect on other people individuals still have the right to do what they think fit. Nor can it be argued that it is not possible for the exercise of these rights to be contrary to the common good, since we do not know all the possible forms that the common good could take. To say, as Amnesty does, that the individual may always exercise these rights is to say that the individual is always right, and that whatever he or she does it cannot be against the common good and thus cannot be a threat to the state. But if in a particular case an individual is wrong, the rights of other people, which it is the duty of the state to protect, are being violated. If a government claims, as they all do, that it is acting for the common good when it restricts an individual's exercise of rights, a political judgement must be made both about the government's claim and about the rightness of the individual's action.

It is easy to think of ways in which people could exercise their freedom of association, assembly, or movement as a threat to the state. In any system of government limits are imposed on them. In Western democracies as well as in totalitarian states, they are defined by law and built into the social system. The freedom of movement of virtually everybody in Britain, for example, is restricted by the existence of vast tracts of privately owned land, from which they are excluded under threat of prosecution. I don't know whether Amnesty would adopt somebody convicted of trespass as a prisoner of conscience, but I doubt whether it would defend the right of a group of workers to associate, by reason of their belief in the wickedness of private property, in order to take over a privately owned industry. Such restrictions are accepted in the West even though they are not in any way intended to further the good of all people. So there is even less reason for saying that there can never be conditions where restrictions may be imposed in order to protect the rights of other people. The fact that one does not believe that these conditions exist anywhere at the present time does not justify the absolute statement that they *cannot*. Merely saying something could be injurious to other people and thus be a threat to the state.

There is something of a contradiction in Amnesty's opposition to any restriction being imposed on freedom of expression. On the one hand, its whole work is based on a belief in the power of public opinion, that is, in the power of the written and spoken word; it can, Amnesty believes, cause even the most oppressive government to change its ways. But, on the other hand, it claims that individuals cannot be a threat to the state and to the rights of other people no matter what they say or write. Again, restrictions are imposed and generally accepted in Western democracies: people are not free to slander or libel others, or to spread alarm and despondency among the general populace in time of war or to undermine the morale of the armed forces. Even if one does not agree with these restrictions (I and, probably, Amnesty would not agree with the last), it is still possible that in other social systems conditions might be such as to justify similar restrictions. If the government claims they are justified, one cannot *assume* they are not. The possibility that such conditions might arise is more remote than it is with regard to the other freedoms but it cannot be absolutely ruled out. It might be claimed that people should still have the right to disagree; but, in practice, those who are imprisoned for conscientiously expressing their views are not simply in theoretical disagreement with their government. They are, and they want to be a threat to a government which identifies its own interests with the good of all; and they probably would not thank anybody for telling them they are not such a threat. Defending their right to be wrong is not of much help to them. The assumption that they are right, however, is just as political as making a judgement about whether or not the government is acting in the common interest.

One cannot avoid deciding who is right – the government or the individual – by claiming that people have an equal right to express their views whether they are right or wrong, that is, whether or not these views are in the interests of the common good. Such a position can only lead one to be indifferent to truth; in which case there is no point in defending even one's own right to one's views. But if you believe that truth is important and that your own views are true, you have not only a right, albeit one limited by the rights of others, to propagate those views, but also a duty to oppose their denial. You can and should recognize, nevertheless, that you are not infallible and so refrain from persecuting others for expressing their views – not only because you are aware that many people whose views were suppressed as dangerous or lunatic eventually turned out to be right, but also because you recognize that the other person is exercising an essential function of a rational human being in searching after truth. In other words, you are tolerant. Error does not have rights; *people* in error do. But there is a great difference between a person's right not to be persecuted for his or her views and having the right to express those views; between tolerance and the absolute right to individual freedom of opinion and expression.

It is sometimes argued (by Hayek, for example) that unless people have the right to express views which are generally considered erroneous, there can be no progress in knowledge. That would be relevant only if there was such a thing as abstract truth and if people were persecuted for thinking it; the views are expressed anyway before they are suppressed. But the reason both for people propagating ideas and for their being persecuted for doing so is the effect which they have on reality here and now. Progress does not come from abstract, academic discussion. And people are persecuted for trying to change the world, not for seeking to interpret it in various ways. The least we can do, which is also the most that can be done apolitically, is to ask that their efforts be tolerated. Tolerance is, and can only be, concerned with the means which governments use to restrict individual freedom, not with their right to do so – that can only be determined in the light of the end for which they impose restrictions. Tolerance means saying, 'Even if these people are wrong, even if they are a genuine threat to the security of the state, and even if you do have the right to restrict them, at least treat them decently.' But one cannot even define 'decently' apolitically. One cannot, as Amnesty does, demand the unconditional release of people who 'are imprisoned, detained or otherwise physically restricted by reason of their political, religious or other conscientiously held beliefs or by reason of their ethnic origin, sex, colour or language, provided that they have not used or advocated violence'.

Anmesty calls these 'prisoners of conscience' and claims that at any one time there are at least 500,000 such prisoners in the world, and that hundreds of thousands of others have 'disappeared' or been killed with at least the connivance of governments. This is a very misleading and confusing claim in that it includes many prisoners who are not prisoners of conscience and excludes many who are.

If the word 'conscience' is to retain any of its normal English meaning, 'prisoners of conscience' must be people imprisoned for doing something knowingly; with awareness of what they are doing and of the consequences of doing it and without prejudicing the rights of other people. Many of Amnesty's half a million prisoners do not fall within this definition. It is doubtful whether any people are imprisoned for such reasons as their ethnic origin or colour. That might be the ideological rationalization of the government concerned, but it is at most an excuse, not a cause. Even if they were imprisoned for that reason, however, this could not be considered a consequence of a conscientious choice about their 'ethnic origin, sex, colour or language'. A notable omission from Amnesty's definition is 'class'. Millions of people are imprisoned or physically restricted because of their class, even when colour or some other factor is given as the excuse. But if people are imprisoned or killed, for whatever reason, without their having consciously said or done anything, they are not prisoners of conscience; they are victims of oppression. An Amnesty publication gives an example – unfortunately typical – of such victims:

> In El Salvador, two married couples and three young children are staying at a friend's house while she is away, when uniformed members of the security forces burst in, demanding to know where the friend is. They torture the adults in front of the children, then beat the screaming children – one aged five – before taking all of them to San Salvador's central barracks. Some days later the children are found in a juvenile reform centre. The adults have 'disappeared' – they have become prisoners of conscience.

But there is no indication that their conscience had anything to do with it. Conscience implies choice; at least, the choice to escape punishment by compromising one's principles or beliefs. They had no choice; they were innocent victims of an oppressive state.

The distinction between 'prisoners of conscience' and 'victims of oppression' is not simply a semantic quibble; it is essential for deciding what action can be taken on their behalf. If people have the right not to be persecuted for expressing their views, they have an even greater right not to be persecuted for doing nothing. Such people are in even greater need of help than those who consciously decide to take some form of action. Further, since they themselves have not expressed any political views nor performed any political actions, demanding that they should not suffer does not involve the making of political judgements. There is no question of having to decide between their views and those of the government on the good of the state, since, by definition, they don't have any. Their right to freedom of expression does not come into consideration; it is a question of their much more fundamental right to be. Once people have exercised their freedom of expression, they are not necessarily 'innocent victims' and, as we have seen, support of them inevitably implies making political judgements. In other words, it is a far more straightforward and apolitical task to provide help for the victims if they are not confused with prisoners of conscience. It is also usually a more urgent one.

If Amnesty, like Humpty Dumpty, is to make words mean what it wants them to mean and is to include in its definition of 'prisoners of conscience' not only such victims of oppression but also, for example, people whose freedom of movement is restricted, then millions more should be added to its total, including the whole black population of South Africa and most of the population of communist states. Further, an untold number of others (nobody bothers even to count them) are excluded because they have 'used or advocated violence', even though they have been constrained by their conscience to do so.

Amnesty's exclusion of these prisoners is at best arbitrary and moralistic, at worst an expression of prejudice in favour of institutionalized violence. The Universal Declaration of Human Rights, which Amnesty seeks to implement, recognizes that if human rights are not protected by law, then man will be compelled, as a last resort, to rebellion against repression and tyranny. One does not oneself have to approve of violence to acknowledge that a person's conscience may demand the use of violence. However, as Paulo Freire says, 'Among the innumerable rights claimed by the dominant consciousness is the right to define violence and to locate it.' Amnesty has exercised that 'right'. It has decided that 'to indulge in symbolic physical acts such as pulling down flags or even defacing posters' (i.e. things which even Amnesty members might have occasion to do) is permissible, as is 'conventional war'. But blowing up power stations, which they are never likely to be called upon to do, is not. With more than a hint of arrogance, Amnesty's 1964/5 Annual Report refers to 'the concern shown by delegates ... to safeguard the use of the term "prisoner of conscience"'. The term was 'safeguarded' by the delegates' unanimous decision not to adopt Nelson Mandela.

It is, if nothing else, an abuse of language to say that Nelson Mandela is not a prisoner of conscience. He would not be in prison at all if it were not for his conscience. He had every opportunity of escaping and securing his own personal freedom but he stayed in South Africa even though he knew that he would eventually be arrested and possibly sentenced to death. He stayed because, as he said from the dock, 'I have cherished the ideal of a democratic and free society in which all persons live together in harmony and with equal opportunities. It is an ideal I hope to live for and to achieve. But, if needs be, it is an ideal for which I am prepared to die.' This was not simply a rhetorical gesture. The words were spoken immediately before sentence was to be passed on him; it was expected that the sentence would be death. Mandela did plan sabotage, though strict instructions were given that people were not to be killed or injured. He did this not 'in a spirit of recklessness, nor because I have any love of violence. I planned it as a result of a calm and sober assessment of the political situation that has arisen after many years of tyranny, exploitation and oppression of my people by the Whites.'

If a person who is prepared to die for what he believes in is not a prisoner of conscience, I do not know who is; but at least I have a less confused idea than Amnesty has. I believe that virtually all prisoners of conscience should be free of any restrictions, because I think they are politically right. As a socialist I would obviously support those imprisoned for opposing a capitalist government, but I also have no difficulty in positively supporting most of those imprisoned in socialist states: firstly, because the practice itself is a sign that it is not a proper socialist state and, secondly, because many of the 'dissidents' are, in any event, more genuinely socialist than their governments. If one is not a socialist one cannot actually support those imprisoned by capitalist governments for advocating socialism; one could only plead for tolerance. But one would automatically support those imprisoned by socialist governments (which is one reason for the disproportionate amount of energy and resources devoted by Amnesty to its work in socialist countries). It is from a political position to the left of that held by any existing government that one can actively support the release of prisoners of conscience in all countries. Some, I think, should be restricted, though not in the way they are. As we have seen, the founder of Amnesty thought, and still thinks, much the same: he conceded that it might be necessary for people to be restricted; it was to the permanence of their imprisonment, the fact that they were 'the Forgotten Prisoners', and to the brutality of the way in which they were treated, that he objected. But if one is not prepared to make *any* political judgement, one cannot say that *any* prisoner of conscience should be released, unless one denudes the word 'conscience' of any meaning. One can, nevertheless, say that all prisoners of conscience should be tolerated and that no victims of oppression should be persecuted. There are limits, however, even to tolerance, limits which for me would certainly not extend to Hayek's 'tolerance for the existence of a group of idle rich'. One may sometimes have not only the right but also the duty to be intolerant. Voltaire allegedly said that the intolerant should not themselves be tolerated. Nowhere perhaps is the need for intolerance greater than in opposing racist propaganda; yet still in Britain today we have people who invoke the concept of freedom of expression to allow such groups as the National Front to propagate racism. No matter how sincerely held people's racist opinions may be, and although they cannot be forced to change them, they do not have the right to express them. This does not make racist views different from any others. It is simply an application of the general principle that individual rights are restricted by the rights of other people. Racism is not a matter of holding bizarre views about other people's rights; nor is it a belief that people are different. People *are* different and I trust they will remain so. Racism, however, defines people in terms of their different racial characteristics and not in terms of their humanity. Although, as I have said, we cannot define precisely what it means to be 'human', racism implies that some people are not human in any sense. Any expression of racism, therefore, necessarily infringes the rights of other people, regardless of whether or not it is likely to lead to violence.

Amnesty spokesmen, however, have said that they would adopt as a prisoner of conscience a person imprisoned for expressing racist views, provided *only* that he or she had not advocated violence. Such spokesmen seem to sense intuitively that it would be wrong to adopt a racist as a prisoner of conscience. Yet Amnesty's absolutist position forces them to come to the opposite conclusion. They therefore indulge in all sorts of tortuous argument to show either that any racist propaganda necessarily involves the advocacy of violence or that in a particular case the person was not actually imprisoned for expressing racist views but because of a legal technicality, and so the question of adoption did not arise. Thus, a publication by the British Section argued that in deciding whether a march by a racist organization should be banned, the danger of violence had to be weighed against the denial of the participants' right to express their views. In the case of Rolf, who was imprisoned for refusing to obey a court order to remove a notice which restricted the letting of his property on racial grounds, it has been argued that his refusal constituted contempt of court; he was therefore imprisoned for that reason and not for expressing racist views.

Since Amnesty claims to derive its authority from the Universal Declaration of Human Rights and the subsequent Conventions and Covenants, it is difficult to understand their confusion and their willingness to protect the 'rights' of racists. The Declaration itself cannot be invoked to defend anyone's right to express racist views since, although its definition of the right to freedom of expression sounds absolute, it is limited by the final article, which precludes the use of the Declaration to justify the denial of any of the rights contained within it. Racist views are aimed at the destruction of the whole basis of the Declaration, which is the recognition of the 'inherent dignity and of the equal and inalienable rights of all members of the human family'. The Covenants and Conventions are even more explicit. The Covenant on Civil and Political Rights states: '*Any* advocacy of national racial or religious hatred that constitutes incitement to discrimination, hostility *or* violence shall be prohibited by law' (Art. 20.2 – my italics).

The Convention on the Elimination of All Forms of Racial Discrimination spells out the prohibition in more detail:

Article 4

State parties condemn all propaganda and all organizations which are based on ideas or theories of superiority of one race or group of persons of one colour or ethnic origin, or which attempts to justify or promote racial hatred and discrimination in any form, and undertake to adopt immediate and positive measures designed to eradicate all incitement to, or acts of, such discrimination and, to this end, with due regard to the principles embodied in the Universal Declaration of Human Rights and the rights expressly set forth in Article 5 of this Convention, *inter alia*:

(a) Shall declare an offence punishable by law *all dissemination of ideas* based on racial superiority or hatred, incitement to such acts against any race or group of persons of another colour or ethnic origin, and also the provision of any assistance to racist activities, including the financing thereof;

(b) Shall declare illegal and prohibit organizations, and also organized and all other propaganda activities, which promote and incite racial discrimination, and shall recognize participation in such organizations or activities as an offence punishable by law (my italics).

Even the non-violent dissemination of racist ideas, therefore, is recognized internationally as a crime. When, however, as Director of the British Section, I asked for a clear statement that Amnesty would not support racists, regardless of whether or not they had advocated violence, I was told, after waiting a year for a reply, that this was 'the ultimate dilemma' and could not be answered. In practice it is answered; and it is answered in favour of nationalists and racists. One former prisoner of conscience, who incidentally had been adopted by a predominantly Jewish Amnesty group, showed himself on his release to be anti-Semitic, anti-Black and in favour of the National Front. The West, he maintained, was far too concerned about the rights of Blacks and neglected Whites; it was good, therefore, to find that in Britain there were people ready to defend the right of Whites to self-determination. There is obviously something amiss when a man like Nelson Mandela is excluded in order to 'safeguard the term "prisoner of conscience" ' for men like that. This is the inevitable result of an unthinking and absolute acceptance of the dictum: 'I do not agree with what you say, but I will defend to the death your right to say it.' Everybody now seems to admit that Voltaire never said that; they should also realize that, even if he did, he was wrong. One should be prepared to die to suppress some opinions rather than to defend them.

Support for the individual's absolute right to freedom of expression is not only an essentially political activity: it can also be a counter-productive one. Amnesty sets out 'to secure throughout the world the observance of the provisions of the Universal Declaration of Human Rights'. Such an aim can hardly be furthered by the defence of the right of people to undermine the very foundation of those provisions by such means as propagating racism or fascism. Amnesty has moved a long way from its original aim of pleading for tolerance of people's ideas and, in adopting a reactionary political position, it limits the effectiveness of what could be done apolitically.

While it is not possible for apolitical activists to go beyond tolerance, it is both possible and necessary to extend the scope of tolerance beyond the defence of people's ideas. Although, in the beginning, Amnesty was at pains to exclude 'men of action', it certainly did not exclude those who had done nothing and yet were being persecuted. One of the first people adopted by Amnesty was a young South African student, Christopher Lindi Payi, who was arrested in São Tomé, when he was on his way to take up a scholarship in Nigeria, and sent to a political prison in Lisbon. According to Amnesty's report, 'He has committed no crime and has not been tried . . . [he] is a victim of political persecution which he has done nothing to provoke.' His arrest certainly had nothing to do with his ideas.

Tolerance means acknowledging that, while the rights of the individual are not absolute, neither are those of the state. The state must, therefore, have some reason for acting against individuals and, even if it has reason, it cannot treat them as it pleases. Tolerance recognizes that there can be a conflict between the rights of the individual and the state, and that this conflict can only be resolved politically; but there can be no conflict if one party has not done anything. If the state acts against someone who has done nothing, it is claiming an absolute right for itself. Deciding whether a person has 'done nothing', however, itself depends upon a political judgement. When, for example, Amnesty reports, 'In the Republic of China (Taiwan), Pai Yatsan was found guilty in November 1975 of "sedition" under the Statute for the Punishment of Sedition, 1949', the putting of 'sedition' in inverted commas implies that, while the government might say it is sedition, Amnesty has decided that it is not and that the man has done nothing. But 'sedition' cannot be defined apolitically. If a British court were to convict someone of sedition, Amnesty would not gainsay it because the court would be applying the same definition as Amnesty does. But what right has Amnesty to impose its politically determined definitions on anybody else?

Liberal democracy is just as much a political ideology as totalitarianism is. To judge people in the light of that ideology is a political activity and it does not cease to be so just because the same norms are applied 'impartially' to both left- and right-wing regimes. Amnesty does indeed criticize governments of both the left and the right, but in so doing it canonizes the centre, where neither truth nor virtue is necessarily to be found. In fact, the centre is the most relative of all positions: in order to remain there you have to adjust your position in response to any movement from either the right or the left. You cannot do that and yet hold absolutist views. If one is concerned about *human* rights in which all share, one does not have to worry about 'balancing' one's activity either geographically or politically.

It is the propensity of governments to lay claim to an absolute right over individuals by treating them as it pleases, rather than by persecuting them for doing nothing, that occasions the possibility of, and need for apolitical action. Maurice Cranston, with reference to Bokassa's reported practice, as self-styled Emperor of the Central African Empire, of personally beating prisoners to death, comments, 'The use of torture at the pleasure of a despot is precisely the kind of thing which Declarations of the Rights of Man are meant to outlaw and which the United Nations at its inception was expected to banish from the earth. This is a matter of moral urgency . . .' (*What Are Human Rights?*, p. 71). It is with such matters of moral urgency that Amnesty and other apolitical human rights activists can and should be concerned. If they were to achieve what the United Nations, despite its professed concern, has failed to do over the past thirty-five years, their existence would be more than justified. If, however, they try to go further, on the basis of spurious political assumptions, their efforts to resolve matters – even of the greatest moral urgency – will be doomed to failure.

Amnesty itself has shown that it is possible, simply by applying moral pressure, to prevent people being killed, tortured or treated inhumanely, without passing any judgement on whether or not they have done anything. I doubt, as I said at virtually every meeting I addressed as Director of the British Section, that Amnesty has ever secured the release of a prisoner from prison; though it has doubtless contributed in particular cases when it also happened to be in the interests of the government concerned to appear to be making concessions to public opinion. Amnesty has never claimed credit for the release of any prisoner. One good reason for this, as an early publication pointed out, is that 'all governments have pride and if they do release a prisoner following Amnesty's efforts and this is publicly gloated upon, they will be less likely to release another one later on. In any case, it is often not a specific outburst by the organization which influences a government, but the steady volume of adverse publicity – both press and radio – reported by its ambassadors abroad.' Most of the prisoners adopted by Amnesty are released after having completed their sentences or as a result of a general amnesty following a change in the political climate. This does not detract from the importance of what has been done, nor from the urgency of what still needs to be done. One cannot do a cost-effectiveness exercise on preventing people from suffering. I am inclined to believe that even if the efforts of Amnesty's quarter of a million members had done no more than save one person from torture, they would have been worthwhile.

It is not Amnesty's task to analyse the nature and causes of this suffering. Its approach was compared by Benenson to that of the Bible, which 'doesn't seek to answer the question "Why does man suffer?", but instead asks in typical Hebrew fashion, "How can we help man in his suffering?"' There is probably as much if not more suffering and oppression now as there was when Amnesty was founded in 1961. It is not possible to make any definitive statement about the comparative degrees of oppression since, firstly, there is no way of comparing different forms of oppression and, secondly, thanks at least in part to the work of Amnesty, there is today much more knowledge (though not necessarily awareness) of what goes on in even the most remote corners of the world. The basic forms of oppression have not essentially changed since the dawn of civilization. Even many of the techniques have a long history. The falanga (the practice of beating people on the soles of their feet), for example, was first mentioned by Demosthenes nearly four hundred years before Christ; and a modern torturer or interrogator would have little to teach Torquemada. Governments are, nevertheless, becoming more efficient in applying the means of oppression. As the means they use have become more sophisticated and more complex so, it is argued, Amnesty has had to adapt the means it uses to achieve even its limited aim. On the other hand, since Amnesty wishes to avoid making political judgements and does not engage in political analysis, and hence does not distinguish between different forms of oppression, it is arguable that for the achievement of its limited aim the simple method of getting as many people as possible to express their disapproval is the most effective one. And, I believe, this has been proved in practice to be the case. Since Amnesty's aims are apolitical, the means used to attain them must also be apolitical; the more complex they become the less possible this is.

A recent survey by the Dutch Section of Amnesty showed that the vast majority of groups relied mainly, in fact almost exclusively, on letter-writing to prisoners, their relatives and the governments concerned. They do this with remarkable consistency, despite the dearth of replies. In the course of a year, groups in the survey made 347 approaches to governments and received only 47 replies. Those working for prisoners in Egypt received no replies from prisoners, their relatives or the government; those with prisoners in the German Democratic Republic, Yugoslavia, Iraq, and the People's Democratic Republic of Yemen heard only from prisoners' relatives. Even more remarkable is the testimony of hundreds of prisoners and their relatives that this actually helps. Some attribute their release to Amnesty, while others, like the wife of a prisoner in Uruguay, express what such support means: 'Every new letter, every word, touches me so much that my eyes fill with tears ... When I feel tired or downhearted, I always return to them. I read and re-read them a thousand times. And with them I always find again the courage to continue.'

During the past twenty-one years, Amnesty Groups have adopted over 20,000 individual prisoners. In addition, individual members and others are encouraged to write each month on behalf of three prisoners who are in especially difficult circumstances. It is estimated that some 20,000 people participate in each of these appeals. Although, as Amnesty itself points out, there may be a certain amount of 'overkill' here, there is evidence that in 30 to 50 per cent of the cases taken up there is at least an improvement in the prisoners' conditions. Amnesty sees this as an excellent 'introductory technique'. The same publication notes that 'it is simple, easily understood and cheap'; but it also achieves all that Amnesty can hope to achieve, so it is difficult to see precisely to what it is 'introductory'.

Amnesty is at its best, and avoids many of the political pitfalls, when it takes emergency action on behalf of any prisoner (not only prisoners of conscience or even political prisoners) who is, or is in danger of being, subjected to torture or whose life is particularly at risk. A whole network (the Urgent Action Network) has been built up so that when such a case arises between 2,000 and 4,000 letters and 200 to 300 telegrams are immediately dispatched from all parts of the world. This results in an improvement in the prisoner's condition in an estimated 40 to 50 per cent of the cases. There is abundant evidence of this. A typical letter from a prisoner's relative reads: 'As many of you already know, the hundreds of telegrams, letters and press reports all over the world succeeded in stopping in the first moment the savage torture to which he was being subjected and saved him from following the fate of many others ... assassinated during the past few months.'

No political ideology makes a virtue out of persecuting people. Many governments freely admit to imprisoning or restricting people, but they claim their actions are justified; they are, therefore, susceptible to moral pressure in particular instances. Few, if any, admit to or seek to justify the practice of torture; it can therefore be opposed wherever it occurs. In 1975 the United Nations adopted by acclamation a declaration for the protection of people from torture and other inhuman or degrading treatment. Since that time, 'Amnesty International has taken action on torture as well as other cruel, inhuman or degrading treatment or punishment in more than sixty countries where government officials inflicted violent measures on people in custody with the deliberate intention of causing them extreme physical and mental suffering.' Several books could be written, based on Amnesty's research, about the incidence of torture. I have no wish, however, either to sicken the majority of readers or to pander to the prurience of the few by recounting the gruesome details. Torture, as Amnesty's submission to the Sixth United Nations Congress on the Prevention of Crime and the Treatment of Offenders points out,

> is not confined to any particular region or political ideology. The victims include men and women, children and old people, political and ordinary criminal prisoners, people engaged in or allegedly engaged in armed conflict and people who have not used or advocated violence. Methods of torture include beatings, mutilations and involve the use of well-elaborated techniques and equipment, both ancient and modern in conception, sometimes designed to make the subsequent verification of torture difficult. Deaths under torture have been common. Torture has taken place in time of war or other emergency and in time of peace and apparent stability.

Although, as the submission continues, torture is most commonly used to obtain incriminating information, 'prisoners have often been tortured as a form of punishment or revenge, to intimidate them or a broader public, to force them to co-operate with the authorities and, in view of the gruesome nature of recent torture techniques, for the sadistic pleasure of their captors'. It is possible that the known torturers are not the worst offenders, bad as they are; the worst offenders are likely to be more efficient in suppressing information about their practices.

In 1973 Amnesty published the first international review of the use of torture. The Preface to the Report stressed that the practice of torture was growing:

> During the last few years the Press has featured stories of torture in South Africa, or Greece or USSR and for a few days the world has been horrified by the account of the brutalities which one group of human

beings, under the protection of the state, has inflicted on another. But this very process of concentrating first on this country and then on that has disguised the most significant feature of the situation: that torture has virtually become a world-wide phenomenon ... What for the last two or three hundred years has been no more than an historical curiosity, has suddenly developed a life of its own and become a social cancer.

The submission quoted above indicates that there has been no noticeable improvement since then. Apart from pleading on behalf of individual victims, Amnesty has also actively promoted the study of the physical and psychological effects of torture and has provided treatment for the victims.

Torture, together with genocide, is in a different category from other violations of human rights; no great political subtlety is required in order to oppose it. National and international laws are incapable of preventing it. Sean MacBride, a former Amnesty Chairman and a Nobel Peace Prize winner, has suggested that the United Nations should have a Commissioner for the Prevention of Genocide and Torture with a free hand and real power to deal with the 'gross and massive violations of human rights involving genocide and torture'. In the meantime, they remain matters of 'moral urgency', to which organizations like Amnesty should perhaps devote *all* their energies. They would, unfortunately, have more than enough to do, and would not need to become embroiled in political arguments. Doubtless more efficient ways of directing these efforts can always be found; but there is no necessary correlation between their effectiveness and their complexity. The simple method of writing letters has proved to have at least some effect.

It cannot, however, be assumed that any appeal to anybody is likely to increase the effect. Namibian activists, for instance, took grave exception to Amnesty groups being encouraged to write to Dirk Mudge, the leader of the Democratic Turnhalle Alliance, since this was seen as recognizing the legitimacy of a body which they considered to be nothing but a puppet of the South African government, which itself was illegally occupying the country. More generally, the question arises when approaches are made to companies operating in the country concerned. Such approaches cannot be made without an ideologically determined position on the nature of capitalism and its relationship with oppression. Amnesty's position is that, unless there is evidence that a company is directly implicated in particular violations of human rights, 'Amnesty does not imply any guilt on the part of a company having economic relations with a government which violates human rights.' It is, therefore, prepared to approach companies in order 'to urge them to use their influence with governments to end human rights violations within AI's mandate'. But not to impute guilt to companies is to imply that they are not guilty; at the very least they are politically neutral, which is precisely what most capitalists would like us to believe. Anyone who has attended the AGMs of banks, which operate in or make loans to oppressive governments, has heard the argument year after year. Some 'progressive' capitalists, like Mr Harry Oppenheimer, go further and claim that economic growth under the aegis of capitalism necessarily leads to political improvements. Some socialists, however, would argue that there is a contradiction in terms between capitalism and the protection of human rights; that oppression is in the interests of capitalism. To assume that companies can have any positive influence is, therefore, an anti-socialist position and an endorsement of liberal capitalism.

Other restrictions are imposed on the method of adopting prisoners and making approaches to governments by the nature of the means which governments use. In an increasing number of instances, the first, and often the last, that anyone hears of the victims is that they are dead or have 'disappeared'.

Most countries in the world have provision in their legislation for the use of the death penalty; only twenty member states of the United Nations have totally abolished it. In some countries it is only imposed for treason or violent crimes; in others it is also used as a punishment for political and economic crimes. In Albania, for example, there are thirty-two offences (of which twenty-three are political or military) which carry the death penalty. Further, as Amnesty's Declaration of Stockholm notes, 'the death penalty is frequently used as an instrument of repression against opposition, racial, ethnic, religious and underprivileged groups'. Amnesty campaigns for the total abolition of the death penalty, considering it to be the ultimate form of torture. Of even greater concern than its continued widespread judicial use is the fact that, as the Declaration also notes, 'the death penalty is increasingly taking the form of unexplained disappearances, extra-judicial executions and political murders'. Amnesty estimates that during the 1970s more than half a million people were victims of political murder.

Such murders take place in many countries, but most notably in Latin America and parts of Africa. They are sometimes perpetrated openly by the government; though, more often, governments deny all knowledge of and responsibility for them, or claim that they resulted from armed combat or from crime prevention. The former category includes

summary executions, ordered by military or political officials for crimes which under national and international law would not warrant a death penalty and/or carried out without provisions for legal procedures or right to appeal. An example is the Red Terror in Ethiopia between 1977 and 1978, when political crimes were referred by the ruling Dcrg to ncwly created urban Kebelle tribunals or to peasant associations, neither of which had any legal experience or offered suspects any legal protection. Kebelle leaders were told to 'spread revolutionary terror', which they did in large part by executing suspected government opponents. In another example, Indonesian occupation forces in East Timor have brutally put down a separatist rebellion there and have apparently executed members of Fretilin (Frente Revolucionario de Este Tinor Independente, or Revolutionary Front for an Independent East Timor) who surrendered under the terms of a supposed amnesty guaranteeing their safety ('Disappearances', AI (USA), p. 85).

These murders are more often carried out

by local law enforcement or military authorities, but not necessarily directly ordered or even approved by the government ... The executions may be carried out by paramilitary groups, associated to varying degrees with official authorities, extremist political parties, or branches of the military or police (examples are the Argentine Anticommunist Alliance, ORDEN in El Salvador, and the Secret Anticommunist Army in Guatemala). They may be committed by vigilante or paramilitary groups loyal to landowners or to other private agencies but with access to police support' (ibid., p. 86).

The fact that such murders have taken place is sometimes flaunted as a means of intimidation. 'In the Philippines, for example, the heads of people executed by the police sometimes have been displayed on spikes to discourage other villagers from political activities. In Guatemala the Press published large photographs of victims whose bodies have been mutilated by death squads, an obvious warning to others whose names are on death lists' (ibid., p. 87).

In all these murders it is at least known that the people have been killed; sometimes it is also known who was responsible. In the case of 'disappearances', no body, official or unofficial, acknowledges responsibility and the fate of the victims is unknown – they may have died under torture, been summarily executed and their bodies disposed of, or be held in a prison or concentration camp. 'The discovery of mass graves of people previously believed to have "disappeared" and the testimony of survivors of secret detention camps have helped not only to fill in the factual vacuum left by each individual "disappearance", but also to refute denials of accountability on the part of government authorities in countries where the practice has become widespread' (ibid., p. 3).

'Disappearances' are usually associated with Latin America. The term was first used (as *desaparecido* in Spanish) to describe a particular government practice applied on a massive scale in Guatemala after 1966, in Chile since late 1973, and in Argentina after March 1976' (ibid., p. 1). (Though Joe Jacobs, writing in *Out of the Ghetto* about the fight against fascism in the East End of London in the 1930s, often refers to his communist comrades 'disappearing'.) In Guatemala there has been a consistent pattern of 'disappearances' since 1966; the toll still rises daily and must now be in excess of 30,000 people. In Chile, according to some sources, 5,000 people were executed in the three months following the coup, and in the following four years more than 1,500 others 'disappeared'. Many of their bodies have since been discovered in mass graves. General Videla, before taking office as President, declared: 'As many people will die in Argentina as necessary to restore order.' In the three years following the coup it proved 'necessary' that some 15,000 people should 'disappear' and that thousands more people should be murdered.

'Disappearances' are not, however, confined to Latin America. In Africa there have been isolated instances in both Black- and White-ruled states: in Kenya, South Africa, Namibia and Rhodesia. There have been allegations of larger-scale incidents of 'disappearances' in times of political crises in the Sudan, Guinea, Zaïre, Cameroon, Central African Empire/Republic and Angola. In Ethiopia, 'disappearances' occurred under the government of Haile Selassie, and thousands of people have been secretly and publicly killed since the provisional military government took power in 1974. Often the first intimation that a person has been killed in prison is when a relative is told to stop bringing food. The number of people who 'disappeared' and were subsequently executed at the hands of Amin's death squads in Uganda may have been as high as 300,000. His namesake in Afghanistan acknowledged that thousands of people had died in custody in Kabul alone. But when he himself was denounced as the murderer he declared that they had simply 'disappeared'. An unknown number of people have 'disappeared' in Afghanistan, and this is doubtless the case in many other countries about which it is difficult, if not impossible, to obtain information.

There is little that Amnesty can do in the face of such massive problems. Its traditional methods can obviously have little effect; polite letters are not likely to deter people from killing in secret. It can, perhaps, through its Urgent Action Network, save some of the victims from the torture to which they are likely to be subjected soon after their 'disappearance'. It can, and does, 'bring attention to the practice itself – what it is, where it is used, by whom and why. In February 1980, for example, national sections of Amnesty International all around the world held a vigil for those who had 'disappeared' in Argentina. Names of thousands of them were read in public places, not only to show that victims of 'disappearances' are not forgotten, but to increase awareness of the problem among the general public' (ibid., p. 148). But, as another Amnesty publication points out, 'International and individual protests will not help to stop "disappearances" and the murder of dissidents. Even an international human rights tribunal, which does not even exist, could do nothing meaningful on the basis of international law. This clearly shows that unusual solutions must be found to put an end to these malpractices and suffering.' Since the document had already pointed out that 'disappearances, executions and systematic torture are not simply phenomena or crimes authorized by politicians, but the result of cruel and anti-human politics', it follows that the 'unusual solutions' referred to must be political ones.

Amnesty is primarily concerned with individuals, though it also campaigns against more general violations of human rights in a particular country. This is even more fraught with political dangers than is the work for individual prisoners. The research on which the campaigns are based is itself necessarily influenced by political preconceptions, which determine which questions are to be asked and the relative importance of the various answers found. Conducting a campaign unavoidably entails political judgements. Amnesty's own guidelines state that it 'must, in its work with home governments, elaborate steps of action (and possible government reactions) with concrete and well-based postulations to the home government on how to use its position in bilateral or international political or economic negotiations on behalf of human rights questions ... evaluations are necessary to find out the possibilities for AI to use the political and economic interrelations between governments ...' Nevertheless, Amnesty does fulfil a very useful function in providing basic information about a large number of countries. Specialized organizations provide more detailed material on particular countries, such as Chile and South Africa, but Amnesty also draws attention to countries which do not have support groups abroad. It thus provides a service to more politically motivated people who can draw their own conclusions from it and decide upon their own course of action. Amnesty can, for example, say 'No to Torture' in Argentina; on its own terms it cannot go on to say, as it did at the time of the soccer World Cup Finals, 'Yes to Football'. That implies a political decision on boycotts, which others might well take.

Realistically, therefore, apolitical activity in the field of human rights is limited to pleas by individuals to other individuals not to torture or ill-treat people. There are some who would maintain that even this is not only a political activity but also a counter-productive one; they believe that people's revolutionary consciousness is raised in proportion to the amount they suffer. This view is usually held by people who are not themselves going to be the ones who suffer; it is *other* people's suffering that will bring about the revolution. It is true that oppressed people are prepared to suffer for their political liberation, and many would prefer to suffer than to exchange their people's political freedom for their own personal comfort. It is not, therefore, for outsiders to negotiate with the oppressors on their behalf and to decide that they ought to collaborate with them in order to save people suffering. Thus Black leaders in South Africa have called upon the West to impose boycotts and sanctions, even though they realize that it is their people who would bear most of the economic burden. They say, as is their right, that they are prepared to pay the price of a comparatively little more suffering because of the long-term political benefits. Western businessmen and politicians, admittedly more out of concern for their own economic interests than for the people, argue that it would be wrong to let people suffer. So, while continuing to make profits, they will enforce 'Codes of Conduct' to protect the poor, helpless Blacks. I am not advocating such an arrogant, patronizing and collaborative approach. There is no collaboration involved in simply demanding that people stop ill-treating other people. In doing this we are helping the perpetrators, as people, as much as we are the victims. Suffering is doubtless part of the struggle of the oppressed, but it surely cannot be 'necessary' for anybody's struggle that people are allowed literally to bash other people's heads in and rip the skin from their faces, to kill unborn children by brutally torturing their pregnant mothers and to massacre thousands of people. That, at least, we can object to without either undue interference in the affairs of another state or, more importantly, without taking away from the people their right to determine their own political destiny.

Amnesty has undoubtedly, though perhaps unwittingly, strayed into the political woods. In doing so, however, it has remained firmly committed to the ideals of Western liberal democracy. It has not, as Bernard Levin for one feared it would, become the tool of communism, despite what the governments of such countries as Guatemala and South Africa and even some of the British conservative media might think. Levin attended Amnesty's first press conference and, although he was left almost speechless by 'so much excellent high-mindedness', he was able to write:

> Of course the communists will use the Appeal for Amnesty unscrupulously, implying that it is behind them in their efforts to get Ambatielos and his like released (which, of course, it will quite properly be) without mentioning the others on whose behalf the organization will be working. The effect of this will be, as it always is where non-communist organizations that admit communist help are concerned, that it will inevitably become suspect to some extent, in the eyes of those who would be inclined to support the campaign's aims over the whole spectrum.

Despite that fear and notwithstanding his scepticism of people who rush to 'turn their swords into platitudes', he concluded, somewhat patronizingly, but magnanimously enough:

> ... its function as a collector and disseminator of information is wholly to the good; its clear refusal to take sides on the political issues involved in these 'conscience' imprisonments is good too; and as a means of helping people otherwise inarticulate to protest and work against injustice it should prove useful (*Spectator*, 2 June 1961).

Its usefulness has lain chiefly in the creation of awareness of the extent and the enormity of human rights violations. The conclusion of the First Annual Report is as true of the subsequent twenty years as it was of 1961/2:

> Perhaps the most important achievement of Amnesty has been that without it peoples and governments would today be *less aware* of how narrow are the boundaries of freedom in at least two thirds of the world; more people would be languishing forgotten behind prison bars; fewer people would be so actively concerned with promoting the basic human freedoms of opinion, religion and of expression; the Universal Declaration of Human Rights would be mouldering in pigeonholes.

The awareness which Amnesty creates, however, cannot be fully expressed through the work of Amnesty. An awareness of the suffering caused by different political ideologies should lead one to question them; it should politicize people and make them realize the need to go beyond Amnesty. Working for Amnesty, or for any apolitical human rights organization, should serve as a novitiate, not as a life-long profession. It cannot be the vehicle for a total political and human commitment. At best, it can inspire people to more direct political activity while giving them the opportunity of relieving the immediate suffering of some individuals; at worst, if it is put forward as a total political solution, it is counter-productive; in between, it may provide a salve for middle-class consciences.

CHAPTER 3

THE UNITED NATIONS'
CONTRIBUTION

If non-governmental organizations like Amnesty can do little about putting an end to persecution and oppression, the inter-governmental ones, to which they look for authority and support, can do even less. Amnesty's own Report on Torture (1975) refers to 'the lamentable record of the Commission of Human Rights in defence of human rights'. More specifically with reference to torture, it says:

> The United Nations has neither effective means nor institutions for dealing with the problem of torture. The most that can be said is that it does provide a number of forums throughout its various organs and agencies in which the problem of torture can be raised. The appropriate division of the United Nations family for this issue is the Commission of Human Rights, part of the Economic and Social Council. Despite its promising title, the Commission has neither the will nor the power to defend the Universal Declaration of Human Rights ... (pp. 71-2).

There is no evidence that there has been any noticeable change since 1975. Uruguay has hardly benefited from being 'listed by the Commission for the past three years as being on its confidential agenda' (AI Annual Report, 1980).

There is no lack of international agreements concerning human rights or of bureaucratic machinery, both at the United Nations and in various regions of the world. But the former still reflect Western dominance and the latter is too cumbersome and too influenced by political factors to be effective, even if there was agreement about what to effect. The United Nations Commission of Human Rights, for example, which consists of forty-three members appointed by governments – and hence subject to political pressures – has been given authority by the Economic and Social Council to investigate 'particular situations which appear to reveal a consistent pattern of gross and reliably attested violations of human rights and fundamental freedoms'. When a complaint is received by the Secretary

General's office it is first sent to a Working Party of the Sub-Commission on Prevention of Discrimination, then to the Sub-Commission itself, and then to the Commission. The Commission may then decide to set up an *ad hoc* investigation committee, which conducts its hearings in secret and does not make its conclusions public. The Commission may finally decide to submit a report to the Economic and Social Council, which has no power to do anything about it. But in the process a lot of people have no doubt been made to feel good and important. This procedure is described by Brownlie (in *Basic Documents on Human Rights*) as 'a great improvement on what went on before 1970'. He admits, however, that it does have many drawbacks and quotes a leading UN official as having commented:

> The procedure appeared to be very promising but due to many procedural technicalities, its time-consuming character and above all the inability or unwillingness of the Commission on Human Rights to act effectively, high expectations made way for strong disappointment. Although official United Nations documentation is silent on this score as a result of the rule of confidentiality, press reports reveal that the Commission on Human Rights saw fit to drop all cases (with the exception of the situations related to the occupied territories in the Middle East and Chile, which were on the public agenda anyway) referred to it by the Sub-Commission (ibid., pp. 15–16).

My one personal experience of the workings of the UN machinery, when I gave evidence to its Special Committee on Apartheid, did nothing to foster any belief in its relevance or efficiency. This Committee is a sort of travelling circus which goes around the world, but not to South Africa, and sets up shop in various centres, complete with such paraphernalia as simultaneous translation equipment for its experts to hear evidence from other experts about South Africa. I spoke about some research I had done, which showed, among other things, that in a fairly typical 'resettlement' area the rate of population growth after ten years was half what it had been when the people were first moved there. What interested them about this was whether this fell within the UN's definition of genocide. The chairman thought it probably did and was quite put out by the fact that I had never heard of the Convention on Genocide. Experts are supposed to know these things; it is not sufficient to have seen people dying. He asked me to study the definition and to write a paper to show whether it did. It did. But apart from providing a neat classification of the problem I fail to see what the object of the exercise was. Nothing was said or done about the practice, but the experts had a word for it. The people are now not just 'dying', they are 'victims of genocide'; but they are still dead.

The problems surrounding the implementation of the various Declarations, Conventions and Covenants, however, are not merely procedural, but follow from the nature of these documents and the political and philosophical assumptions underlying them. The United Nations was established in an attempt to prevent a repetition of the atrocities of two world wars. A cynic might be tempted to feel that nations which themselves had been prepared to drop atomic bombs on innocent people were hardly in a position to 'reaffirm their faith ... in the dignity and worth of the human person'. Nevertheless one of its aims was 'to achieve international co-operation ... in promoting and encouraging respect for human rights and for fundamental freedoms for all without distinction as to race, sex, language, or religion ...' (Art. 1.3). Several other references to human rights are made in the Charter and the members pledged themselves to take joint and separate action in co-operation with the UN to ensure respect for them. Since then the UN has, as Brownlie says, 'given impetus to the development of standards concerning human rights ... [it] has undertaken both general propaganda work and the burden of drafting legal instruments containing detailed provisions'. And that is where the problems start.

Its first detailed statement was the Universal Declaration of Human Rights (1948), which seeks to cover everything from the right to life to holidays with pay. The Declaration, though often regarded as the most authoritative document on human rights, is simply a statement of intent and is not legally binding even on those who signed it. It has nevertheless acquired a moral authority and, since it is an explication of the obligation contained in the UN Charter, it could be argued that states bind themselves to it by becoming members of the UN. Legally binding or not, the standards it sets are essentially Western and its detailed provisions are meaningless or contradictory.

There has long been criticism of the Western, liberal, democratic bias of the Declaration from people of the Second World, whose UN representatives abstained when the Declaration was voted on, and from those of the Third World, who were scarcely represented at the United Nations in 1948. Edison Zvobgo of Zimbabwe, for example, says: 'There was never any doubt that the "human rights" that the United States, France, Britain and their allies sought to universalize were those that were consistent with their own values and traditions' (Kommers and Loescher, *Human Rights and American Foreign Policy*, p. 91). Roosevelt, he considers, sought to make the world 'more Western if not specifically American'. He points out that, among other things, the Declaration seeks to impose free enterprise and capitalism on the rest of the world, to outlaw one-party states and to universalize Western-style elections. Although he comments particularly on economic rights, he also objects to the 'Rousseau–Lockean' view of man on which the whole of the UN Charter and the Declaration are based. For an African, he says, an individual in isolation only has potential rights, which become actual in relationship with other people. The Western bias, therefore, is not only political; it is also philosophical. This is further evidenced in the assumption on which the very attempt to prescribe universal norms is based: that it is possible to lay down general principles which can govern particular actions.

Unless one is to allow a completely subjective morality and thus have no grounds for condemning the actions of even the Hitlers and Vorsters of this world, one must have some general principles. It is not possible, however, for a general principle to take account of the almost infinite variety of circumstances which may surround concrete actions. One cannot, therefore, deduce from a general principle what should be done in a particular case. 'Thou shalt not steal' is a general principle, but it is of no use in determining what constitutes stealing in a particular instance. If it is stealing it is wrong, but is it stealing? Thus both Thomas Aquinas and John Locke accepted the principle 'Thou shalt not steal', but Aquinas concluded that a starving man had the right to take what he needed from a man who had more than he needed – taking what belonged to another was not in this case stealing; while Locke, although he thought that the rich man might have the duty to give to the poor man, still considered that the poor man would be stealing if he helped himself. (This is also consistent with the individualistic view of man: the right to property is vested in the individual.)

General principles must, of their nature, be so general and vague as to have no immediate practical application. What can be deduced from general principles are moral or ethical imperatives, which only apply in certain given circumstances. The medieval proscription of usury was a moral imperative derived from the principle 'Thou shalt not steal'. It might well have been valid, given the role of money in that economy; it cannot, however, remain valid whatever the nature of the economy.

The Declaration and many of its interpreters tend to confuse general principles and moral imperatives. Articles 1–12 are general principles, which can offer no guidance in practice. No one could take exception to such statements as 'Everyone has the right to life, liberty and security of person' (Art. 3), or 'Everyone has the right to recognition everywhere as a person before the law' (Art. 6); but there can be widely differing, and equally valid, practical conclusions drawn from them. The other articles are moral imperatives for Western-type societies. All the Declaration is saying in these articles is: given that the Western, liberal, democratic society is the ideal form of society, these rights should be accorded to people. And that is all it can say. It cannot give any guidance about what you should do if you happen to believe in some other form of society, since it *assumes* the normative value of Western society. The Declaration itself implicitly acknowledges this when it allows that the exercise of the rights mentioned may be limited by law, not only in order to protect the rights of others, but also to meet 'the just requirements of morality, public order and the general welfare *in a democratic society*' (Art. 29.2; my italics).

Other forms of society might accept the general principles – which can all be summed up by saying that people have the right to be treated as people – but not the specific moral imperatives. There is nothing contradictory in states accepting the Declaration and not accepting our interpretation of it. To invoke the Declaration against these societies, one would have to show that their actions violate the general principle of the inherent dignity of people, not simply that they are contrary to a particular provision of the Declaration. It cannot be argued, for instance, that the Soviet Union's practice of imprisoning political dissidents is a rejection of the principle laid down in Article 9: 'No one shall be subjected to arbitrary arrest, detention, or exile.' It would be if it were arbitrary, but the principle itself can throw no light on the question of whether or not it is.

> In terms of communist values and institutions, the coercion and interference to which the dissidents are subjected is not arbitrary. There are good reasons for it. It is the duty of the communist citizen loyally to follow the directives of the Communist Party in all political matters. To challenge the political leadership of the party is to proclaim oneself an enemy of communism. That is what the dissidents have done, which is why they are in trouble. They have not, of course, done anything wrong in terms of the values and institutions of liberal democracy, but a communist state is not a liberal democracy (A. J. M. Milne in Dowrick (ed.) *Human Rights, Problems, Perspectives and Texts*, p. 35).

The practice might still be wrong, but if it is, it is because something is wrong with communist values and institutions, not because it contravenes the Universal Declaration of Human Rights.

The Declaration does not, as Martin Ennals, Amnesty's General Secretary for twelve years, claims, confirm 'Amnesty International's *absolute* belief that despite differences of environment, human rights are universal'. It simply makes the same false assumption that 'Western' and 'universal' are synonymous. If the Declaration were to be fully implemented throughout the world, it would mean the imposition of Western standards on the rest of the world. It is as well, therefore, that the UN machinery is either unable or unwilling to do so. Nevertheless, the general principle enunciated by the Declaration remains valid. While a government is not always obliged to act in a liberal democratic manner and to believe, for example, that the private ownership of property is essential to a person's dignity, it is never justified in treating people as less than people – whatever that might mean. The Declaration thus merits two cheers, as Milne says, 'one for the fundamental principle that all human beings are fellow human beings. Another for the idea of human rights as a minimum standard. But I think that we should withhold the third cheer because of the paradox in the Universal Declaration and because of the danger that the idea will degenerate into a slogan' (ibid., p. 36). It has degenerated into something worse than a slogan when it is used to defend the right of racists to spread their propaganda.

Since the adoption of the Universal Declaration, the United Nations has adopted numerous legally binding Conventions on specific issues, such as genocide, refugees, the rights of the child, racial discrimination and discrimination against women. It has also adopted two Covenants of a more general nature: one on Civil and Political Rights, the other on Economic, Social and Cultural Rights. These spell out the provisions of the Declaration in more detail and attempt to take some cognizance of the existence of non-Western states. Professor James Fawcett suggested many years ago that there were strong arguments against continuing to recognize the Universal Declaration as the basic human rights instrument and for the view that it has been replaced by these Covenants. According to Brownlie, they were intended to supersede the Declaration, since they 'have undoubted legal force as treaties for the parties to them'. Only about half the member states, however, are party to them.

Neither the Declaration itself nor the Covenants take such an absolutist view of individual rights as Amnesty, which does not 'accept a contradiction between the rights of peoples and nations on the one hand and the human rights of individuals on the other. Human rights have many times been violated in the name of so-called higher interests, such as the "nation", the "party" or the "struggle".' It is not clear from his writing whether John Locke believed that man did once actually live in a 'state of nature'; given his fundamentalist Christian beliefs, he probably did. Man, according to Locke, could only enjoy full individual liberty in such a state, which Amnesty seems to believe still persists. Though Locke realized that, happy though that state might have been, it had certain drawbacks, such as the lack of a 'common measure to decide all controversies' and the absence of a 'known and indifferent judge, with authority to determine all differences according to the established law'. So man formed himself into a society, and 'the power of doing whatsoever he thought fit for the preservation of himself and the rest of mankind he gives up to be regulated by laws made by the society, so far forth as the preservation of himself and the rest of that society shall require; which laws of the society in many things confine the liberty he had by the law of nature'. Mill, too, who is often regarded as an advocate of absolute individual liberty, accepted that 'every law and every rule of morals is contrary to liberty. A despot, who is entirely emancipated from both, is the only person whose freedom of action is complete. A measure of government, therefore, is not necessarily bad because it is contrary to liberty; and to blame it for that reason leads to confusion of ideas' (Dworkin, *Taking Rights Seriously*, p. 262). Hayek, who admits to having 'represented those guarantees of individual freedom as if they were absolute rights which could never be infringed', acknowledges that 'even the most fundamental principles of a free society, however, may have to be temporarily sacrificed when, but only when, it is a question of preserving liberty in the long run, as in the case of war . . . even such fundamental rights as freedom of speech may have to be curtailed in situations of "clear and present danger".' One cannot avoid making political judgements about the wrongness of the measures taken by governments by claiming that, whether they are politically right or wrong, they are necessarily an infringement of the rights of the individual. The UN documents recognize that there are 'higher interests', and that the state has the right to limit the rights of its citizens by law. These limitations virtually and necessarily negate the usefulness of the documents for all practical purposes. The Covenant on Civil and Political Rights, for example, states:

> In time of public emergency which threatens the life of the nation and the existence of which is officially proclaimed, the State Parties to the present Covenant may take measures derogating from the obligations under the present Covenant to the extent strictly required by the exigencies of the situation, provided that such measures are not inconsistent with their other obligations under international law and do not involve discrimination solely on the grounds of race, colour, sex, language, religion or social origin (Art. 4.1).

There have been prolonged states of emergency in many countries throughout the world in recent years – Uruguay, Argentina, Guatemala,

Rhodesia, Brunei (where it has been maintained since 1962), to name a few – as a cover for the suppression of political opposition. As long as the emergency is 'officially proclaimed', the authority of the Covenant cannot be invoked against the extraordinary powers which the governments assume. A judgement on the legitimacy of the proclamation, which is the crucial issue, cannot be derived from the Covenant.

The Covenant does attempt to limit the power of the state even in times of emergency, by adding in Article 4.2: 'No derogation from Articles 6,7,8 (paragraphs 1 and 2), 11, 15, 16 and 18 may be made under this provision.' These articles concern the following rights: to life (Art. 6); not to be subjected to torture or to cruel, inhuman or degrading treatment or punishment (Art. 7); not to be held in slavery or servitude (Art. 8); not to be held guilty of an offence which was not an offence at the time it was committed (Art. 15); to recognition as a person before the law (Art. 16); and to freedom of thought, conscience and religion (Art. 18). The right not to be imprisoned merely on the grounds of inability to fulfil a contractual obligation (Art. 11) does not seem of any great relevance.

Some of these rights, like the provisions of the Declaration, are simply statements of general principles. The fact that one's right not to be *arbitrarily* deprived of life cannot be derogated does nothing to determine the meaning of 'arbitrary'. A government which kills people during a state of emergency would not claim that it was justified in derogating from Article 6; it would simply say that the killing was not arbitrary and so it had not contravened the Covenant. In any case, Article 6 allows for the 'sentence of death to be imposed only for the most serious crimes in accordance with the law in force at the time of the commission of the crime'. All a government has to do in order to avoid violating the Covenant is pass a law declaring that certain actions are most serious crimes punishable by death.

The Article on freedom of thought may not be derogated from, but the article itself provides that the right may be limited to 'protect public safety, order, health or morals'. Further, Article 19 states that the right to freedom of opinion and of expression (which is the main source of conflict between individuals and the state, and is the primary concern of human rights organizations like Amnesty) may be restricted, whether or not there is a state of emergency, 'for the protection of national security'. 'National security' is the most widespread excuse for suppressing political opposition; and it is certainly not confined to communist countries. It is true also of South Africa, of military dictatorships in Latin America and of repressive regimes in general. If a right, which is already severely limited by the rights of others, may be further restricted in the interests of national security, public order, public health and morals, there is not much point in laying claim to it. Hedged around with such limitations, it does not really matter whether the relevant articles of the Covenant can be derogated from or not.

All that is left from the Covenant of any importance, therefore, is the prohibition of torture and the non-derogation of the right of people not to be subjected to it. Such a bald statement of principle has not had, and is not likely to have, any effect on the practice. It does not, of course, solve the difficulty of defining torture in practice. No matter what means they use, torturers do not 'torture'; they carry out 'investigation in depth' or 'civic therapy' (cf. AI Report on Torture, p. 34). And some people have rather esoteric notions about what constitutes torture for other people. I met a parent at Eton College who considered that chopping a person's hand off was a very appropriate punishment for theft; but chopping both off was going too far.

It is possible to conceive of, though not perhaps to imagine or to consider, circumstances when what is normally considered torture is not torture as a dehumanizing practice – victims may have already dehumanized themselves; but for all practical purposes the prohibition of torture may be considered an absolute one. This is a moral rather than a political judgement. The right not to be subjected to it is recognized not only in the Declaration and the Covenant but also in the Declaration of the Citizen's Rights in the Arab States and Countries, and in the European and American Conventions on Human Rights. It remains, however, 'a right without an international remedy' (ibid., p. 71).

The UN has adopted a Declaration on Protection from Torture (1975) which simply states the general principles, and has requested the Commission on Human Rights to draw up a Convention in the light of these principles. Given the history of other Conventions and the impossibility of implementing them (either because of their internal contradictions, vagueness, or alleged universality, or because of the absence of an effective will on the part of UN organs and member states), the precise terms of any further Convention are of little consequence. The Commission's efforts so far (August 1981) appear to be concerned with the protection of the state rather than the victim. Thus the proposed definition of torture excludes actions which are sanctioned by a court; such actions could include blinding, public flogging and amputations. This would mean, in effect, that the state could torture, and only unauthorized individuals would be prevented from doing so. Further, if people who claim to have been tortured wish to gain any redress or to prevent statements made being used against them, they will have to prove that this was done deliberately and not by mistake, which is almost impossible. The Commission has also set up a Working Party to deal with the question of 'disappearances'. Its first report to the Commission in 1981 named fifteen countries where the practice had occurred. The Working Party is not able to conduct its own investigations; it simply collects information from other sources and then seeks to resolve the matter in co-operation with the government concerned. Since 'disappearances' are, by definition, cases where the government explicitly denies all knowledge and responsibility, this is hardly likely to achieve very much.

The setting up of working parties and commissions is at least an official recognition of the gravity of particular problems; it generates some awareness of the plight of people and it provides a focus for the work of non-governmental organizations. But the legal documents which eventually issue from them can always be circumvented, either genuinely, because one does not accept Western norms, or at least with the aid of a little casuistry; even if they couldn't be circumvented, oppressive governments would not be deterred by legal obligations which carry no effective sanctions. The imposing of effective sanctions would not be in the interest of the major powers; they would have no one to whom to sell their military equipment and 'repressive technology'. In any event, states can always decline to become party to conventions which might prove inconvenient for them.

Countries which adhere to Western norms have no difficulty with the Universal Declaration or with the Covenants, since these deal with rights that can be encapsulated and defused in a Western society. Most of the Conventions deal with specific issues which no longer directly concern Western states. They can, therefore, make great play of the fact that other countries are guilty of such crimes as religious intolerance, rendering people stateless, and genocide; and that socialist countries in particular do not observe the Declaration. They are not so vociferous concerning Conventions which have been adopted through the influence of Second and Third World countries and which do challenge Western practice. Thus in 1973, as a result of a proposal from Guinea and the Soviet Union, the UN adopted the Convention on the Suppression and Punishment of the Crime of Apartheid. No non-communist state has become a party to it; the United States and the United Kingdom joined Portugal and South Africa in voting against the Resolution which authorized it.

The United States claimed that the new Convention was 'not necessary in view of the broad, all-inclusive provisions of the International Convention on the Elimination of all Forms of Racial Discrimination'. 'Broad, all-inclusive provisions', as we have noted, are harmless and meaningless, and so the United States could accept them; they were not prepared to be more specific. The earlier Convention did condemn apartheid, in passing, as a form of racial discrimination. Apartheid is, however, much more than that. It is a systematic regime not only, not indeed primarily of racial discrimination, but also of economic exploitation and political domination. The latter Convention itself assumes the liberal, racial analysis of apartheid, but it does refer to the 'exploitation of the labour of a racial group or groups'.

More importantly, it goes on to state that 'international criminal responsibility shall apply, irrespective of the motive involved, to individuals, members of organizations and institutions and representatives of the state ... whenever they ... directly abet, encourage or co-operate in the commission of the crime of apartheid'. Investment in and trade with South Africa are, therefore, according to the Convention, quite literally 'criminal'. Whether those responsible are themselves racists or not; whether their only motive is to make money – which is normally a justification for any action according to Western standards; or whether they profess to be concerned about improving the lot of Blacks, is all irrelevant. 'Irrespective of the motive involved', they are co-operating in the crime of apartheid, because apartheid, as it is presently practised in South Africa and not as an abstract political theory, necessarily demands the exploitation of black labour. There is no business or commercial enterprise in South Africa which does not benefit from the apartheid system; if not by directly using exploited labour, at least from the low taxation which is a consequence of its use by others. By declining to become parties to the Convention, Western states have the consolation of knowing that, while they are committing what most other nations consider to be a crime against humanity, they are not actually breaking an international law. They can, while retaining their great respect for law, continue to trade with, and invest in, South Africa and block any attempts to impose international sanctions. Ultimately, the economic and political interests of the West are more important than all the Declarations, Covenants and Conventions of the United Nations, and they determine whether these can have any effectiveness.

Regional agreements, like the American and the European Conventions on Human Rights, avoid many of the inherent drawbacks of international ones, since they are entered into by governments which, as the European Convention notes, 'are like-minded and have a common heritage of political traditions, ideals, freedoms and the rule of law'. They are able to agree on the 'collective enforcement of certain of the Rights stated in the Declaration'. They do not seek to impose new norms but only to deal with aberrations from, or anomalies in, an agreed system. The European

Convention, which was signed in 1950 and came into force in 1953, was the first attempt 'at giving specific legal content to human rights in an international agreement, and combining this with the establishment of machinery for supervision and enforcement' (Brownlie, *Basic Documents on Human Rights*, p. 242). The 'machinery' – that is, the European Commission of Human Rights, the European Court of Human Rights and the Committee of Ministers – is, however, 'excruciatingly slow. More than two years passed before the Council's [of Europe] Commission of Human Rights compiled and published its report on Greece and, more recently, its report on the 1971 allegations of torture in Northern Ireland took five years to reach publication' (AI Report on Torture in Greece, p. 6).

The European Commission was at least more actively concerned about the torture in Greece during the colonels' regime than was the UN Commission, which was even more ineffective than usual because of the United States' interest in defending Greece. The European Commission's report did finally succeed in having Greece expelled from the Council of Europe. This is probably the most dramatic action that has been taken in pursuance of a Convention. Yet, as the Amnesty Report on Torture comments, 'in terms of the international protection of human rights, the Greek case pushed the available international remedies the furthest yet, but these alone were clearly insufficient to stop the practice. Where power counted, in the US government, the Report was nearly ignored' (ibid., p. 98). The torture continued, as did American military and other aid.

Whatever their nature or number, international agreements can do nothing actually to prevent the violation of human rights. Amnesty's remarks about Greece are true of all other issues: 'To analyse the problem of torture in Greece in terms of articles of international agreements violated might be an interesting theoretical exercise but it would miss the point. The issue can only be understood in terms of a total political reality; these agreements themselves only have meaning in terms of reality' (ibid., p. 80). (The authors of this Amnesty Report, incidentally, appear to have no inhibitions, as members of an apolitical organization, about making very political judgements!)

The Declaration and the Covenants, which are considered the most important documents, offer no practical help either in defining or defending the rights of people. Nor are they of any help in establishing priorities. In fact, their position on the relationship between the recognition of human rights and the establishment of a just social order is a contradictory one. On the one hand, the preamble to the Declaration states that the 'recognition of the inherent dignity and of the equal and inalienable rights of all members of the human family is *the foundation of freedom, justice and peace in the world*'. On the other, Article 28 says: 'Everyone is entitled to a social and international order in which the rights and freedoms set forth in this Declaration *can be fully realized*.' The same contradiction is found in the preamble to the Covenant on Civil and Political Rights. It first virtually repeats what the Declaration says about human rights, but then goes on to say, 'in accordance with the Universal Declaration of Human Rights, the ideal of free human beings enjoying civil and political freedom and freedom from fear and want *can only be achieved* if conditions are created whereby everyone may enjoy his civil and political rights, as well as his economic, social and cultural rights' (my italics). The Covenant on Economic Social and Cultural Rights says the same. This is not a question of the relationship between different kinds of human rights, but of whether the recognition of any or all individual rights leads to or follows from the establishment of a just social order. The Declaration and the Covenants answer, 'Both'.

Human rights activists, as opposed to those concerned only with tolerance, presumably believe that respect for human rights is the cause rather than the effect of an improved social order; otherwise there would be no point to their activities. This is, in fact, part of the conventional wisdom of the Establishment. The Brandt Report, for example, having established the need for a new international order, concludes that it is not the lack of technical resources which prevents the challenge being met, but rather the fact that the necessary political decisions 'will not be possible without a global consensus on the moral plane that the basis of any world or national order must be people [so far so good] and respect for their individual rights, as defined in the Universal Declaration of Human Rights. Only if these ideas are sincerely accepted by governments, and especially by individuals, will the political decisions be possible and viable' (p. 268). Such a view is based on an essentially individualistic understanding of society and implies that the violation of human rights is a moral rather than a political problem.

I myself, when working for Amnesty, believed that the rights with which Amnesty was concerned were so minimal that everybody could be expected to observe them and that their recognition was a prerequisite for any just political system. Such recognition was a first step which everybody could and should take together, even if with the next step they went their several ideologically determined ways. This is true, however, only of the general principle contained in the Declaration and not of its specific provisions.

To believe that persuading governments to desist from their repressive practices and recognize individual rights will lead to the establishment of a more just order is to imply that these practices are ends in themselves; governments get some sort of kick out of ill-treating people. But people do not dehumanize other people because they are evil; they are evil because they dehumanize other people. Repressive practices are means to an end, the end being the maintenance of some form of political power. If the violation of human rights is a means to an end, their recognition can only be achieved as an effect of a change in the end; it cannot be the cause of such change.

The means which oppressive governments use – imprisonment, execution and torture – are often obviously wrong. Some of them would be wrong however good the end the government was pursuing. Not because they are absolutely wrong, but because an end cannot be realized by means which contradict it. There is nothing either Machiavellian or Jesuitical in a proper understanding of the dictum that the end justifies the means. (John Stuart Mill, for example, accepted it: 'Despotism is a legitimate mode of government in dealing with barbarians, provided the end be their improvement and the means justified by actually extending that end' (On Liberty)). Every moral human action must, by definition, have an end; it is the end which determines both its human-ness and its morality. An act which is simply a 'means' cannot, therefore, have a morality. Cutting off a leg might be either a means of cruel torture or a life-saving operation; it depends solely on the end or purpose for which it is done. The dictum does not mean that a good end justifies any means; but it does mean that if the end is wrong then any means, no matter how humane, is also wrong.

It is pointless, therefore, from the point of view of overcoming oppression, simply to try to persuade governments to be more humane in the means they employ. In any event, this may succeed only in persuading them to find other means which, because they would be less susceptible to criticism, would be even more effective for oppressing people. What is wrong with a country like South Africa is not so much that it has the Terrorism and Internal Security Acts, which provide for indefinite detention without trial, as that the system is such that it needs such Acts. It is the system which needs to be changed rather than the means used to implement it. And it would still need to be changed even if political opponents were entertained in five-star hotels rather than locked up in prison.

It is a contradiction in terms to ask a government which depends for its existence on the restriction of individual rights to concede these rights without changing its political system. Even Amnesty does sometimes acknowledge that this is so in practice, though it claims to have 'a common and constant position: we neither oppose or support any government or political system'. Its Report on Torture in Brazil, for example, states:

'Torture is a manifestation and *necessary result* of a political model, with a judicial and socio-economic framework ... The entire apparatus exists to carry out torture, with *no other justification* than the maintenance of the present regime.' To oppose torture and imprisonment in such a country is to oppose its political system. If one accepts that the system needs to be changed, one cannot reasonably expect this to be brought about as a by-product of moral objections to the means presently employed. Campaigning against the violation of human rights *is* a subversive activity. It cannot, therefore, be effectively undertaken either by voluntary organizations which seek to make themselves acceptable to all governments by insisting that they are impartial and apolitical, or by United Nations Commissions which depend on the co-operation of the governments concerned.

CHAPTER 4

INDIVIDUAL AND
HUMAN RIGHTS

It is no longer true, as it was in 1961, according to Peter Benenson, that if
you 'open your newspaper any day of the week you will find a report from
somewhere in the world of someone being imprisoned, tortured or executed
because his opinions or religion are unacceptable to his government'. The
practice still goes on, but most cases, unless they concern well-known Soviet
dissidents, are not reported. Everybody has heard of Andrei Sakharov; but
who has heard of Wu Yueh-ming, who has been imprisoned in the Republic
of China (Taiwan) since 1951, after having been charged with 'having been
handed a Communist Party poster and having posted it up', and with
'having joined a communist group'? Nelson Mandela is news; George
Ramafoku dying of cancer in a remote camp was not. Clare Frances
Wilson's torture in Chile was only news because she had a British con-
nection; had her father not been born in England, her name and her fate
would have passed unnoticed at the tail-end of an Amnesty press release.
It is not only Amnesty's habit of burying the main news item in about the
fourth paragraph that accounts for most of its press releases not being
picked up. News editors, as I have been told, have grown weary of hearing
from 'international do-gooders' who keep telling them much the same story
with only the name of the country changed, and people are not interested
in countries which were not even mentioned in their geography lessons. We
can cope with a few martyrs – in fact we almost welcome them as vicarious
sufferers on our behalf. Too many make us feel guilty.

In virtually every country of the world there are individuals and minority
groups who are being persecuted in varying degrees: Blacks in Britain;
Catholics in Northern Ireland; Baptists, Pentecostalists, Seventh Day
Adventists, and nationalist groups in the Soviet Union and other socialist
states; Jehovah's Witnesses in Greece; Shiites in Iraq; religious sects in
Ethiopia, Malawi and Zambia; the Haratine in Mauritania; communists in
capitalist countries; and deviationists in socialist countries. In many
countries it is the majority which is oppressed and persecution is the norm.

Amnesty International's 1981 Annual Report lists 117 countries; almost without exception the entries begin with the statement that Amnesty is concerned about the detention of political opponents without trial and the imprisonment of people after unfair trials. One exception is Guatemala, where the dominant concern was 'that people who opposed or were imagined to oppose the government were systematically seized and frequently tortured and murdered by both uniformed and plain-clothed members of the security forces'. Amnesty's latest catalogue of persecution fills 400 pages and would be even longer were it not for the impossibility of obtaining any information at all about many countries. It does demonstrate yet again, as other reports over the past twenty years have done, the unfortunate truth of Benenson's contention that 'there is no area of the world where people are not suffering for their beliefs and no ideology which is blameless'.

There are two ways of dealing with political criticism: either you can allow people to indulge in it as freely as they want and then ignore it; or you can take it seriously and suppress it. The more entrenched in power a government is and the less difference there is between it and its opponents, the more easily it can afford to take the former course. That, generally speaking, is what happens in the rich, capitalist countries of the north. I will return later to the question of oppression and persecution in 'advanced' capitalist and socialist countries. Here I am primarily concerned with persecution in the rest of the world,* not because it is worse but because it more clearly illustrates the point I wish to make.

It is not possible to give even a glimpse of the total picture of such persecution. I want simply to illustrate, rather than to analyse, the scope of the problem and the different forms which it takes and to examine the relevance of a concern for individual rights. While I do not wish in any way to minimize the importance of preventing even one person from suffering, it is important, I think, to distinguish between sporadic, even though fairly numerous instances of persecution, and the systematic practice of it against large sections of the population. The latter is part of a wider pattern of oppression, whereas the former is not. There is widespread persecution of both types throughout Africa, Latin America and Asia.

In Africa, excluding South Africa and Namibia, most of the persecution is related to actual or threatened coups, and the victims tend to be the previous or potential political leaders. (Amnesty has, for example, appealed for the release of three former presidents in Benin; it has investigated the

* Note: The quotations in the following pages are taken from AI Report, 1981, as are most of the figures.

cases of the former Head of State and of three associates of the former president in the Congo; and it has adopted the former Prime Minister of São Tomé and Principe.) It would be patronizing and untrue to suggest that this is due simply to the fact that forty-six of the forty-eight countries concerned have only obtained their independence since 1945. (Liberia, which has been independent since 1847, has had similar problems; and Ethiopia, both under Haile Selassie and the provisional military government, has hardly been a model of tolerance.) There are other more important factors, such as the precarious economic condition most of them were left in by the colonial powers and their continued dependence on the same powers; the reluctant granting of independence after long periods of internal strife; and the arbitrary way in which the continent was divided up by the colonialists in the first place, with complete disregard for traditional boundaries. One can at least sympathize with the anonymous president quoted by Edison Zvobgo: 'Imperialists talk about human rights, drinking tea or sipping champagne. They can afford to – after all, they have it made. If we had had slaves for 200 years to build our roads, build our homesteads, sow our fields; if we had had multi-nationals for 300 years looting wealth from other people's land ... we too could talk about human rights from our air-conditioned offices and homes' (Kommers and Loescher, op. cit., p. 97).

It is sometimes argued, either as part of a general racist theme or, in particular, as a defence of continued White rule in South Africa, that the people in independent African states are worse off than they were under colonial rule. Economically their fate is not really in their hands; it remains in the hands of their erstwhile masters. As a rule, they do not practise systematic persecution and they are no match for their white brothers in the South as far as sheer brutality is concerned. There are, nonetheless, some unfortunate exceptions, even apart from Idi Amin who, while being admired by many Blacks for his ability to treat the Western powers with scorn, is generally regarded as an aberration. In recent years the two other worst offenders, Macie Nguema of Equatorial Guinea and the self-styled Emperor Bokassa of the Central African Empire, have also been overthrown. A coup in Guinea-Bissau in 1980 revealed that the previous government of President Cabral had been little better and had been guilty of 'serious and repeated violations of human rights'. The new government released at least a hundred prisoners who had been secretly detained. It also announced the discovery of mass graves in various parts of the country containing some 500 corpses of people who had either been shot by a commando unit or asphyxiated in prison. The departure of these oppressors is undoubtedly an improvement, but it would have been surprising had there not been recriminations against those who participated in the atrocities perpetrated during their regimes. Some of the offenders, regrettably, are still in power. In Guinea, for example, it is feared that the number of prisoners is approaching the level of the early 1970s when, between 1971 and 1976, thousands of political prisoners were arrested and some opposition sources claim that as many as 4,000 of them died in prison. Amnesty has also expressed grave concern about the detention and treatment of prisoners in Zaïre.

The fact that countries do not necessarily improve with age is amply demonstrated in Latin America, where systematic persecution is the norm in countries which have been 'independent' for up to 150 years. The wholesale killing of people in Guatemala and El Salvador has thrust itself upon our attention; we have even been treated to television pictures of bodies twitching as soldiers forced their victims to lie on the ground and then shot them. In Argentina they dispose of thousands of people a little more secretly but just as effectively. Conditions in Chile have, according to the British Foreign Office, improved sufficiently to justify the resumption of diplomatic relations and the sale of arms. They are only 'better' compared with what they were at the height of the repression following the coup in 1973. There are, in fact, indications that Chile is returning to that state. Amnesty, in 1980 and 1981,

> received numerous allegations of torture by the security forces. A consistent pattern emerged from the detailed reports: agents of the CNI, the army or the navy seized people in their homes or on the street; they took them, blindfolded, on the floors of vans or cars to torture centres in military barracks or secret locations. There, they were interrogated and tortured for days at a time: commonly with the *parilla*, a metal grid to which the victim is tied while electric shocks are administered. Severe beatings, threats and humiliation were also reported ... More people have died as a result of torture at the hands of the security forces or in so-called 'armed confrontations' with them.

Guatemala, El Salvador, Argentina, Chile – their gruesome history is well known. There is not perhaps such an awareness of systematic repression in other Latin American countries. I once introduced a trade unionist from Colombia to a foreign affairs spokesman of one of the main political parties. He was not too sure where Colombia was, but thought that it was 'one of the good places in Latin America'. In fact, the trade unionist wanted to tell him about the arrest of two thousand of his colleagues in the preceding couple of months. In 1980 Amnesty published a detailed report on Colombia which documented abuses by government forces including arbitrary arrests, torture and the unexplained killings of peasant and Indian leaders in rural areas ... The report emphasized that the state of siege in force almost continuously for thirty years and recent special security laws had facilitated human rights abuses by security forces ... [it] cited more than 600 individual cases ... It also described Colombian army establishments where torture was alleged to have been practised ... The report paid particular attention to abuses of power in the extensive rural areas under military control, the so-called 'militarized zones'. Security measures intended to combat active guerilla opposition groups affected the peasant population as a whole through 'continual searches, detention and the use of torture ...' which created an atmosphere of 'permanent threat and terror'.

Bolivia is known for the dire poverty of the people who work in the tin mines. Since the coup in July 1980 there has also been widespread and overt political repression, particularly of trade unionists. In the four months following the coup between 1,500 and 2,000 people were detained without trial; many more were expelled under the threat of death; many others were killed by the army or paramilitary groups. 'Sweeping arrests were reported in towns and industrial centres throughout Bolivia. In the mining areas ... where strikes against the coup had been organized, troops attacked with tanks and heavy weapons to put down any resistance to the military takeover ... Since the coup, most political and trade union leaders have been exiled.'

In Haiti, 'almost all independent journalists, broadcasters, human rights activists, lawyers defending political detainees and opposition leaders in the country were arrested or expelled during 1980, putting an effective end to the already limited rights to freedom of assembly, association, expression and information'. Given all that, and the varying degrees of repression in other Latin American countries such as Mexico and Paraguay, it is difficult to give much credence to the view expressed by Mr Nicholas Ridley, when Minister of State at the Foreign Office, that Cuba has the worst human rights record of any country in the world, though it is true that there are a number of prisoners in Cuba who have been imprisoned for fifteen or more years and that tens of thousands of people have chosen to leave the country.

Political repression in many Asian countries is marked not only by the large numbers involved – which must, of course, be seen in relation to the total population – but also by the length of time that people are held. At least one prisoner in Taiwan has been in prison since 1946 and more than thirty others have served thirty or more years. Some 70,000 people were detained during the nine years when a state of martial law was in force in the Philippines; while nearly 33,000 were arrested following the coup in Indonesia in 1965. Of these latter, at least 300 were still in prison in 1981 and thousands of those who had been released were still subject to certain restrictions. In Malaysia and Singapore, too, hundreds of people detained in the early 1960s were still being held. In Brunei, which is still officially under British protection, there are only nine, who had been detained since 1962; but nine in Brunei is the equivalent of 10,000 in China. Even tiny Vanatu managed to arrest a thousand people in the four months following its independence.

Since the end of the war in Vietnam in 1975, 40,000 people have been sent to 're-education camps' even though they have not been found guilty of any crime. The original decree provided that they should be held for three years, but 26,000 were still being detained in 1981. Amnesty considers this to be 'incompatible with internationally recognized standards and basic principles of justice'. The Vietnamese government, however, believes that 'the system of re-education without trial as applied in Vietnam is the most humanitarian system, and the most advantageous one for law offenders. It is also in accordance with the tradition of generosity and humanitarianism of the Vietnamese nation and the loftiest ideals of mankind.' Thousands of people are similarly held in Laos.

It is possible that there are countries where persecution is even more widespread and systematic than in those mentioned; on the other hand there are countries in both Latin America and Asia where it is at worst only sporadic. I am aware that there are whole areas of the world that I have not mentioned: Iran, where over 2,000 people were executed between June and October 1981, and the Middle East in general; the genocide in Kampuchea. The examples given are, however, sufficient to show that when we speak of persecution we are not talking about present-day Galileos; few, if any, of those concerned were interested in propounding world-shattering ideas. They were simply, but vehemently, opposed to the government that happened to be in power. People in the West are rightly concerned about the inhuman way in which these people are treated – some even recognize the West's responsibility for much of it. But such opposition and the consequent persecution have little to do with the Western conception of individual rights, and nothing can be done about it on that basis.

It might appear somewhat preposterous, or even absurd, in the face of such an unimaginable amount of human suffering, to introduce philosophical considerations. This is not an attempt to evade the issue. I believe that we cannot even understand, let alone help to solve, the problem if we see political repression simply as the multiplication of individual violations of human rights. I do not believe that this is the primary concern of either the governments or, more importantly, of the victims themselves; and if it is not their concern, there is no reason for it being ours. The wrongness of the 'resettlement' of two million Africans in South Africa, for example, does not lie in the fact that the right to freedom of movement of two million people has been violated. I never heard anybody complain about that; what they did complain about was that their children were dying. They did not really have freedom of movement in the first place, since their place of residence was determined by the possibility of obtaining a livelihood there. The government was not concerned with their moving about either; it was interested in making them available as a source of cheap labour and in preventing them from organizing themselves politically. The physical mobility of any one individual out of the two million was no threat at all to the government; the threat came from their being part of a subject people from whom all political power must be withheld. Likewise, when the government in Bolivia arrests a trade unionist it does not do so because it has anything against that particular individual; it is because it is worried about the trade unionism in which the victim is interested.

There are of course people who, because of their particular position, ability or actions, are the personal target for government reprisals. Such people form only a tiny minority of those being persecuted. It is with them, however, that the West is primarily concerned; perhaps because, not surprisingly, most of them are in socialist states, which do not share the West's preoccupation with individual rights. Thus Amnesty notes that among the thousands of people who had been held in re-education camps in Laos were the former Director of the National Bank, a former diplomat and *chef de cabinet*, and the former Director of the National Agricultural Institute; among the hundreds detained in Malaysia were the former Assistant Secretary General of the Labour Party, two former Deputy Ministers and a couple of professors. Such people are not, as Amnesty claims, 'the tip of the iceberg'. Their position is qualitatively different from that of the millions of anonymous ones. I am not suggesting that we should not be concerned about their welfare. I am only saying that they are not necessarily representative of the majority and that the latter cannot be helped simply by a multiplication of the efforts that are made on behalf of the former. Members of previous governments and their associates are often arrested, as in many African countries, even when there is no systematic persecution or oppression. When such people are arrested, and thousands of others are arrested at the same time, the two events are not necessarily part of the same process. Focusing attention on them, therefore, does not begin to tackle the problem of systematic persecution – and certainly not that of oppression, of which such persecution is a manifestation.

Debate about human rights usually centres around such questions as the origin and nature of rights – whether they derive from natural or positive law, from God or society; the relationship between political and civil rights on the one hand, and economic and social rights on the other; the conflict between individual and collective rights. There are many political and economic reasons for Western philosophers and political theorists being concerned about such questions; we will examine some of them later. I am concerned here with a more fundamental question, which concerns all rights, political and economic: namely, whether they are 'individual' or 'human'. To talk of individual human rights is a contradiction in terms; they must be one or the other.

My individuality is something I possess; it is that which differentiates me from other people and makes me unique. Our humanity is something that we have in common; that which we share with everybody else. If rights are the preserve of individuals, it is not possible for everybody to have them since they could not at the same time belong uniquely to each person. Even if it were possible for everybody to have them, they would be useless, since there would be nobody to recognize them: everybody would be concerned with their own. We are individuals and we do have the right to develop our own individuality; but not by arrogating to ourselves that which is common to all. Concern for individual fullness of life leads, among other things, to complete solitude, as Dostoyevsky saw:

> Everyone strives to keep his individuality as apart as possible, wishes to secure the greatest possible fullness of life for himself; but meantime all his efforts result not in attaining fullness of life but self-destruction, for instead of self-realization he ends by arriving at complete solitude. Everywhere in these days men have, in their mockery, ceased to understand that the true security is to be found in social solidarity rather than in isolated individual effort (*The Brothers Karamazov*).

If rights are human, that is, something shared, nobody can have any one of them fully unless everybody else does; my share is necessarily smaller, the smaller the whole. That is why freedom, for example, is indivisible, not because each individual has an equal right to it in its totality, but because we all share in the totality.

The Western liberal tradition has sought to evade the issue of the indivisibility of human rights either by talking of rights which are irrelevant to most people or by limiting the definition of 'individual' to members of their own class or group; the others are simply 'the masses', whether they be Blacks, women or the poor. John Stuart Mill doubtless considered himself to be one of the 'exceptional individuals, [who] instead of being deterred, should be encouraged to act differently from the mass'. The individual freedom which he was at pains to defend has nothing to do with human rights and it is not his fault that it has been interpreted in that way. In his essay *On Liberty*, Mill was only dealing with an individual's right to perform actions 'in so far as these concern the interest of no one but himself'. A modern example would be refusing to obey a law which made the wearing of seat-belts compulsory: not an issue which is of burning interest to the two thirds of the world which is starving. There are very few such occasions; fewer than Mill would have allowed. Even getting drunk, to use one of his examples, can also affect other people – dependants, doctors and society as a whole – if it impairs the person's ability to make the contribution of which he is capable. But to extend Mill's principle to all individual actions is to trivialize gross violations of human dignity. The offence caused to Mill by a government which decided that the genitalia of statues should be covered with fig-leaves hardly bears comparison with the offence caused to a person who has electrodes attached to his own genitalia. To condemn both these actions as violations of the same principle is to trivialize the latter. Torture is wrong, not because it violates the same principle that would allow a person to refuse to wear a seat-belt, but because it violates the inherent dignity of a person, which wearing a seat-belt does not. It is the humanity, not the individuality, of the person which is at stake.

The Western tradition has been primarily concerned with the right to individual liberty and that in only a very restricted sense. While there is no justification for Europeans to 'speak as if the concept of freedom, born in Greece, perfected in Christianity and realized in practice through institutions developed by the English, the French, the Americans and other Western people were Europe's gift to the world' (Plamenatz, *Man and Society*, vol. I, p. 45), freedom of conscience as the right to hold and profess what principles we choose and to live in accordance with them is an essentially Western concept. It was with this concept that the spiritual progenitors of the modern human rights industry were concerned and it is with this that many people confuse human rights. John Locke was not the first to formulate the doctrine of liberty of conscience, but it is his version which is generally accepted as the most authoritative and which has had the most influence. He was primarily concerned with religious liberty, which he was not very keen on extending to atheists or Roman Catholics, but once that was granted it followed that people were also free in other matters, all of which were considered less important than religion. Such liberty was for Locke a natural right of man, based on the 'law of nature'. It was the task of government to protect that right by formulating laws which were 'common to everyone of that society'. But 'everyone', for Locke, meant only the educated and propertied classes. 'Whoever, in his day, put a value on freedom put a value on what in practice could be enjoyed fully only by a small part of the community. Locke claimed for all men what he could hardly have denied, had he been seriously challenged, was still within the reach of only a few' (ibid., p. 249). One means of protecting this right was peasant ownership of land. But, as Bertrand Russell remarked, 'He seems blandly unaware that, in all the countries of Europe, the realization of this programme would be hardly possible without a bloody revolution ... The odd thing is that he could announce doctrines requiring so much revolution before they could be put into effect, and yet show no sign that he thought the system existing in his day unjust, or that he was aware of its being different from the system that he advocated' (*A History of Western Philosophy*, p. 659). It was not different for Locke himself or for the other individuals about whom he was concerned.

Although those concerned with human rights may not be consciously aware of the influence of Locke, it was he who established the concept of individual freedom of conscience, and 'where it is established, it is apt to be considered the most precious of all freedoms' (Plamenatz, p. 49). It is so considered by the defenders of individual rights. But just as it was of no benefit to most people in the unequal society of Locke's day, neither is it the primary concern of most people today. Laws 'common to everyone' are of no help if either the laws themselves are instruments of repression or if those who come under the law are unequal in every other respect. The right to individual liberty of conscience means little either to an unemployed black girl in Toxteth or to the people being killed in Guatemala. It is not what oppressed people themselves mean when they speak of freedom and liberation. When Gustavo Gutierrez says, 'A broad and deep aspiration for liberation inflames the history of mankind in our day, liberation from all that limits or keeps man from self-fulfilment, liberation from all impediments to the exercise of his freedom', he is talking about freedom 'as a historical conquest'; this means to 'understand that the step from an abstract to a real freedom is not taken without a struggle against all the forces that oppress man ... The goal is not only better living conditions, a radical change of structures, a social revolution; it is much more: the continuous creation, never ending, of a new way to be a man, a *permanent cultural revolution*' (*A Theology of Liberation*, p. 32). Such a revolution will not be furthered by the repetition of the tired clichés of traditional Western liberalism, nor simply by trying to shock people into action by the graphic description of particular abuses. 'The old notions of civil liberty and of social order,' said Lord Acton, 'did not benefit the masses of the people ... Society, whose laws were made by the upper class alone, announced that the best things for the poor is not to be born, and the next best, to die in childhood, and suffered them to live in misery and crime and pain' (Quoted in Goodman, *A Study of Liberty and Revolution*, p. 109). Any newer ones, such as those contained in various bills of rights, do not seem to have been much of an improvement.

In addition to the vast amount of political repression to which we have alluded, albeit very sketchily, the people of the South, in particular, are also subject to economic oppression, which affects even larger numbers. The differences between the North and the South are summarized by the Brandt Report:

> The North including Eastern Europe has a quarter of the world's population and four fifths of its income; the South including China has three billion people – three quarters of the world's population but living on one fifth of the world's income. In the North, the average person can expect to live for more than seventy years; he or she will rarely be hungry, and will be educated at least up to secondary level. In the countries of the South the great majority of people have a life expectancy of closer to fifty years; in the poorest countries one out of every four children dies before the age of five; one fifth or more of all the people in the South suffer from hunger and malnutrition; fifty per cent have no chance to become literate (p. 32).

As long as we are concerned with individual rather than human rights, and as long as this concern is based on an essentially Lockean view of liberty, we cannot tackle either of these aspects of oppression; we can be concerned, at best, about only a relatively privileged minority, whether these be the rich or even well-known prisoners of conscience. This is illustrated by a comment in Amnesty's 1981 Report. It notes that 'throughout the year armed hostilities involving foreign troops continued in three territories – Afghanistan, Kampuchea and East Timor. In each, human rights violations of concern to Amnesty have been reported, in some cases involving both sides in the fighting.' It concludes, with pure bathos, 'however, the nature of these conflicts has critically hampered investigation of human rights abuses'. It also 'hampered' the very existence of several hundred thousand people.

It is only possible to prescind from one set of rights and to concentrate on another if you consider that all rights are entities which can be possessed in their entirety by individuals, rather than shared in by people. People cannot fully share in the right to freedom of expression, for example, if they are too hungry to be bothered about it, or even if they are illiterate; and even more so if they are dead. There is not simply some undefinable relationship, or even a purely politico-economic one, between political and economic oppression. Oppression, like freedom, is indivisible, because it is human beings who are suffering. If people are reduced to a less than human condition economically, they *cannot* be treated as fully human politically, and vice versa. People are either human or they are not; and either we are all fully human or no one is. At present it is rather obvious that none of us is. It is not so obvious, but it is equally true, that we all can be.

I would not entirely agree with Marx that 'the philosophers have only *interpreted* the world, in various ways; the point, however, is to *change* it'. After all, as I think Heidegger pointed out, how are you to know that the world needs changing unless you have interpreted it? Human rights organizations do, therefore, perform an essential task in providing information about violations of human rights; the problem lies in allowing a particular interpretation of that information to determine what action should be taken. It is, nevertheless, true that the ways in which the philosophers have interpreted the world are various indeed, and have done little to improve the lot of the vast majority of mankind.

Philosophy does play a part, consciously or unconsciously; it is important, I believe, to question the philosophical as well as the political assumptions underlying the preoccupation with individual rights, since they can vitiate a genuine concern. The claim by human rights activists that any philosophizing is irrelevant owes more, I am sure, to Burke than it does to Marx. One can reject any philosophy or political theory, as Burke did, because it is threatening to the conventional wisdom which supports the status quo and one's own privileged position within it; or, as Marx said he did, because truth can only be found in practice, not in abstractions. Much of the activism is in fact based on philosophy in the sense that Marx rejected it, while Marx's own philosophy is rejected as an attack on freedom; whereas all that it attacks is Western liberal individualism, and a philosophy which assumes that there are ready-made principles in the light of which one can decide what to do. The individualist can deal with his brother at a distance, as an object of concern, but not as a fellow subject; he can study him, but he cannot learn with him. Amnesty, for example, believes that 'objectivity' is a virtue. In evaluating its methods of working and in developing new ones, it says, 'It is important that the evaluator and the operator are different people – this guarantees greater objectivity in the final product'; which means that one should not allow one's actions to be influenced by what is actually happening. You must stand aside and consider them in the light of some abstract principles.

The individual freedom which Western liberal philosophers have debated is not the concern of the mass of people, and the mass of people are not the concern of the philosophers. We need to be aware of the influence of this philosophy and to reject it in order to replace it with a more genuinely human one. Political philosophies are not just dreamt up by some eccentric individuals. They have a very practical purpose: namely, to justify a particular political order. Political systems are based on certain assumptions, which may or may not be valid and which further the interests of certain groups. The philosophy explains and give credibility to the assumptions and thus justifies the pursuit of these interests, which its exponents share. This was probably more important when politicians needed to have policies, rather than simply programmes, and when they had to convince people themselves, rather than leaving it to Saatchi and Saatchi. Nevertheless it does still have an influence, though more in the form of assumptions than in conscious application. Liberal philosophy seeks to justify what is – namely, the privilege of the few. We need a philosophy which is concerned with what *should be* – for all.

I am not suggesting that we must first formulate a perfect theory before we can do anything about the horrendous problem of oppression; though even that would be preferable to 'the irrational fanaticism of crusades'. But as Freire says, 'whatever the degree of action on the world, it implies a theory . . . We must have a clear and lucid grasp of our action (which implies a theory) whether we wish to or not' (*Education for Critical Consciousness*, p. 112). Freire himself is an eminently practical man, as his pioneering work for adult literacy in Brazil and Chile shows. He recognized that teaching people to read and write was not simply a matter of technique; the methods and texts used are based on a philosophy of man, which determines whether the process leads to further domestication or to liberation. This is equally true of campaigning for the recognition of human rights. It is not simply a question of finding the most efficient way of dealing with the symptoms. The basis for planning action, says Freire, is 'the interrelation of the awareness of our aim and of process . . . which implies methods, objectives and value options' (ibid., p. 22). We would not be helping the oppressed if we were to find the most highly efficient means of instilling in them a Western understanding of the rights of man, which is based on an almost exclusive emphasis on man as an individual. At best, individualism leads to the practice of 'assistencialism' (a term used in Latin America to describe policies of financial or social assistance, which attack symptoms but not the causes of social ills) which Freire describes as 'an especially pernicious method of trying to vitiate popular participation in the historical process ... it contradicts man's natural vocation as subject in that it treats the recipient as a passive object'. It leads to the pacification of people rather than to their liberation. Analysing the value options underlying concern for human rights is not, therefore, simply an academic exercise.

Individualism rejects our common humanity and sees concern for others, if at all, as a work of supererogation, and even then it only extends to other individuals. According to Hayek, we can only be concerned about people we know: 'While we can feel genuine concern for the fate of our familiar neighbours, we cannot feel in the same way about the thousands or millions of unfortunates whom we know to exist in the world.' Of course we cannot if we see them simply as millions of other individuals. The ultimate expression of an individualist philosophy is: Each man for himself.

But if human rights are indivisible, working for their realization cannot be a separate concern, let alone an optional extra; it cannot be separated from our other personal and political concerns. We are not working for rights for others, but for human rights. We are not fulfilling a moral obligation to others; we are fulfilling our own humanity. To the Western ear a 'common humanity' might sound like a vague, unreal, metaphysical concept. To some, however, it comes quite naturally. If you tell a Zulu that some misfortune has befallen somebody, the immediate response will not be a wishy-washy 'Poor soul', or even a crude but possibly more affectionate 'Poor sod', but '*Hau Bantu*' – 'Oh, people', or even '*Our* people': the two conversants share in the suffering of the third person. There is more truth than perhaps even he himself realized at the time in Peter Benenson's advice to Amnesty office workers: 'Amnesty will be as successful as those who work for it retain their cheerfulness, and as influential as they themselves practise its principles.' 'Its principles' need some re-examining, but the sentiment is valid.

CHAPTER 5

THE ROOTS OF OPPRESSION

Underlying all debate or activity concerning human rights are assumptions, even convictions or beliefs, about the nature of freedom and equality, which in turn depend on a view of man. Questions about the relationship between freedom to exercise political and civil rights, on the one hand, and equality in the enjoyment of economic, social and cultural rights, on the other; or about the relative degree of importance which should be attached to them, only have any relevance within an individualistic understanding of man and his rights. They do not arise when we are dealing with *human* rights because these are inseparable, not only in theory but in practice. In practice it does not happen that while some people have greater individual liberty, the others have greater economic prosperity. On the contrary, a minority enjoy both and the majority have neither. The only relevant question is: Why is there a minority and a majority and can we do more than change the proportions? It is irrelevant to that majority that, as Roger Plant concludes in his study of Guatemala, 'it may be said that there are two levels of the human rights debate: civil and political freedoms at one level, and national and international economic justice at a deeper level. Which ranks first depends mainly on one's political ideology' (*Guatemala: Unnatural Disaster*, p. 118). It is irrelevant in fact to everybody because, as he continues: 'Meanwhile, it is certain that the urban and rural poor in a country like Guatemala have all of these rights violated at the same time.' If that is the reality, as it is in all oppressive countries, there is no point in debating something else; and the question of priority is at best a theoretical question within the framework of a liberal ideology. If all people had equal political freedom they would also have economic equality, since no one would have the means of taking advantage of anybody else. Likewise, if everybody was economically and socially equal there would be no need to restrict anybody's political freedom. This would necessarily mean restricting the individual freedom of the minority, but it could not be seen as a restriction of their *human* right. Since 'human-ness' is a common possession and constitutes a common standard (how else do you know something is human other than by the fact that it is common to all individuals?), nobody can claim a greater share of it as a human right. Whatever other claim they might make to it, it cannot be based on their human-ness. But, the liberal will say, people are not in fact equal in all respects and the recognition of this necessarily leads to inequalities, at least in the economic and social spheres: some are cleverer, some more cunning, some more competitive, some of higher birth or education. True, but the very fact that these belong only to some people demonstrates that they are individual, not human qualities. Their presence or absence, therefore, has no bearing on a person's claim to human rights.

The fact that all people are equally human does not mean that they are all the same, as Hayek seems to think it does. 'Nothing,' he says, 'is more damaging to the demand for equal treatment than to base it on so obviously untrue an assumption as that of the factual equality of all men. To rest the case for *equal* treatment of national or racial minorities on the assertion that they do not *differ* from other men is implicitly to admit that factual inequality would justify unequal treatment; and the proof that some differences do, in fact, exist would not be long in forthcoming'(*The Constitution of Liberty*, p. 86; my italics). But the opposite of 'equal' is 'unequal', not 'different'. He goes on to defend the importance of individual differences as a justification for inequality. 'The boundless variety of human nature,' he observes, '. . . is one of the most distinctive facts about the human species.' That is true of the distinction between the human and any other species. It cannot, however, be true of the distinction between people since, if the distinctive fact about people was the way in which they differed from one another, we would have no way of deciding who belonged to the human species. He quotes with approval from R. J. Williams's *Free and Unequal: The Biological Basis of Individual Liberty*: 'As a result of nature and nurture the newborn infant may become one of the greatest men or women ever to have lived. In every case he or she has the makings of a distinctive individual . . . If the differences are not very important, then freedom is not very important and the idea of individual worth is not very important.' Hayek himself continues, 'The writer justly adds that the widely held uniformity theory of human nature, which on the surface appears to accord with democracy . . . would in time undermine the very basic ideals of freedom and individual worth and render life as we know it meaningless.' The obvious response is: Does life as we know it have any meaning anyway, when two thirds of the population are hungry and the other third are threatened by annihilation by nuclear bombs? I have never heard of the uniformity theory, but I have not said that human nature is uniform; only that it is something in which everyone has an equal right to share. Further, the statement that 'if differences are not very important then freedom is not very important', is only true if 'freedom' means the defence of individual differences. It does not, therefore, say anything; it is a self-fulfilling prophecy.

Equality does not undermine individual worth; it assesses it differently: in human rather than individual terms. For Hayek, there is little point in liberty unless it demonstrates that 'some manners of living are more successful than others' – regardless of the cost to other people of this 'success' (ibid., p. 85). But who decides what is 'successful'? If it is defined by those who believe in the paramount importance of the individual, it will necessarily be defined in terms of individual privilege and wealth. If, however, an individual is seen primarily as part of humanity, 'success' will be measured in terms of service to society and the reward will not have to be of a material kind.

For the individualist there cannot be freedom and equality for everyone; since the distinctive individual qualities which are preserved by his understanding of individual liberty inevitably lead to inequality. Only those who possess the same *individual* qualities have the right to be treated equally. Hayek, it is true, is an extreme individualist, but he does at least have the merit of making explicit the assumptions on which any individualist approach is based. Those who exalt individual liberty at the expense of equality; those who, like Dahrendorf (in *Social Inequality*, edited by André Béteille), believe that 'the idea of a perfectly egalitarian society is not only unrealistic; it is terrible', are those who are quite satisfied with the way things are – for them. To justify their privileged position they equate the status quo with the natural order.

For the vast majority of people in the world, the status quo is one of oppression. One of the great dangers of simply providing people with more and more factual information about the extent of oppression is that the more effectively this is done the more it is likely to confirm people in the view that there is something natural about this state of affairs, despite the obvious contradiction involved in it being natural to do something which is generally regarded as inhuman. People are disposed towards that view because it saves them doing anything about the problem. If it is true that the poverty, suffering, anxiety and other consequences of inequality are, as Dahrendorf says, the result of 'historical and therefore, in an ultimate sense, arbitrary forces that erect insuperable barriers of caste or estate between men', this would seem to provide an excuse for doing nothing, rather than 'an impetus towards liberty'. If the barriers are by definition insuperable, the only reason for attacking them could be the masochistic pleasure derived from hitting one's head against a wall, or the relief which follows when one stops.

If we are to be part of the efforts to overcome oppression, or at least not to hamper those of others, we must look beyond an explanation of the immediate facts. One response to these facts is simply to deny responsibility: it's nothing to do with me. This implicitly or even explicitly denies that man can do anything about changing the world and is based on a deterministic view of history: oppression has always taken place so it must happen; it is part of the natural order of things and, whether it continues or not, is part of the same order, so there is neither the need for nor the possibility of doing anything. This is a classical conservative position and its influence is seen in other areas: no one is to blame for such phenomena as unemployment and poverty; they are the inevitable workings of the 'natural' law of supply and demand and other hidden forces. Those who adopt such a position have a view of reality without morality. Others attribute 'the facts' to the aberrant behaviour of certain individuals. They have a morality but they do not see reality as something which can be really changed. They implicitly accept the ideology of the status quo, since from what are the culprits straying but the norms already laid down by us? They can therefore only engage in essentially reformist actions like condemning individual violations of individual rights, or even in tilting at windmills, albeit with the greatest zeal and with highly sophisticated weaponry.

It cannot be part of the natural order of things that some men are oppressors, because they have nothing in common that would explain it. They are not all capitalists or all socialists; they are not all Whites or all Blacks, nor all Christians or all Jews. What they do have in common is that they are all human beings, but they have that in common with everybody else, including the oppressed. Why should an alleged natural tendency to oppression manifest itself in the oppressors rather than in the oppressed? Some would reply: Because the oppressed have had no chance; if they obtained power they would be just as oppressive as their present oppressors – look what has happened in so many countries in Africa and Asia; you can't change human nature. So runs the popular application of Western philosophy, which is a philosophy of despair – except for those who are quite happy with the present reality. This philosophy, as I said earlier, is only concerned with explaining what is. It is not concerned with what should be.

This philosophy has also led to a distorted interpretation of Christianity, which is then used to legitimize the present order: because what is, is, what should be has to be postponed to another world. We cannot, therefore, overcome all suffering and oppression and have a perfect society in this world. We cannot, according to this 'theology', have all that and heaven too. But we can. If we are concerned with changing the world, we must be convinced that it can be changed radically, not just improved. If 'human nature' precludes radical change, it precludes all change. If we can achieve any change at all, we are not dealing with human nature in the static sense in which it is understood in Western philosophy. In that sense there cannot be degrees of human nature: what is, either is or is not.

One of the distinctive features of man is that he is able to *act* contrary to his nature; but he cannot act unnaturally *because* of his human nature. The question is: Why do men sometimes *choose* to act in an inhuman way? It cannot be argued that, given that man has the power to choose, it is inevitable – part of the natural order of things – that he sometimes chooses wrongly. It can only be shown that this has always happened, not that it must and always will happen. It happens because, although man is essentially a rational creature, he is *not yet* a perfectly rational creature and his development towards that state is hindered by the fact that he lives in an irrational, because inhuman, society. Christian theology does not postpone the fullness of this development to heaven. In fact it has nothing to say about the nature of heaven; it is concerned with the future of this world and with the possibility of it being totally transformed. It gives no encouragement to the prophets of doom.

The practice of oppression can only be considered 'natural' if human beings are seen essentially and exclusively as individuals. But that does not get us very far. It means that certain people oppress because that is the way they are; there is still nothing we can do about it. The fact that some people are inclined to do certain things does not prove that either the tendency itself or its consequences are natural. Western philosophy is prone, on the one hand, to blaming all the evils of the world on natural tendencies and thus ridding its proponents of any responsibility for them, and, on the other, to justifying other practices, which it considers desirable, on the same basis. Thus, we are told, the right to private ownership of property derives from man's natural acquisitiveness. Since the right is based on human nature, any inequality which follows from it is also part of the natural order. It is not explained how, in the process, selfishness is transformed into a virtue. If the desire to have is indeed part of human nature, then theft is an equally legitimate expression of it. But it is individuals who desire to have and, since this desire can only be fulfilled at the expense of other people – by stealing from them in one way or another – it is essentially anti-human. Such anti-human activity cannot provide the basis for a natural or human right any more than the inhumanity of oppression can be accounted for in terms of natural tendencies. We should not concern ourselves with such contradictions in terms; we should rather be concerned about the contradictions between what is and what should be in reality.

Those who use 'human nature' as a justification for the status quo, and as an excuse for not doing anything about it, dismiss the possibility of a perfectly free and equal society as utopian. It is utopian, but it cannot be dismissed. 'Utopian' does not necessarily mean 'impossible of realization'. The earlier meaning, and the sense in which I use it, was 'ideally perfect in respect of politics, laws, customs and conditions'. The qualification was added later – no doubt to rationalize the lack of progress towards the realization of such a state. But if perfect freedom and equality is not a realizable ideal, there is no reason for seeing any degree of freedom or equality as desirable. There cannot be even a partial realization of something that cannot exist. Those who claim to dismiss 'utopia' do not in fact dismiss it; they are claiming that it already exists in their own isolated individual world.

The remoteness of the prospect of 'utopia' is not part of the natural order of things, nor can it be attributed to the individual qualities (or lack of them) of the oppressors, since their distinctive individual qualities are mutually exclusive. It is possible to find white and black oppressors who have all the same individual qualities except their colour. But colour cannot be the explanation for both groups. If Whites oppress because they are white, why do Blacks do it? It cannot be said that Whites do it not just because they are white but because they are white capitalists, since there are also black capitalists who are oppressors.

Oppression is a universal phenomenon, not only in its extent, but also in its nature. It cannot, therefore, be combated by a piecemeal attack on its particular manifestations, which is the approach of those who are concerned only with 'methods' and not with 'objectives and values'. Efforts to convert the oppressors by persuading them not to perpetrate particular abuses might create a few new men, but it is not part of 'the gradual conquest of true freedom which leads to the creation of a new man and a qualitatively different society' (Gutierrez, A Theology of Liberation, p. 36). It is rather like trying to abolish the institution of private property by persuading as many people as possible to give it away. It might still be worthwhile, just as persuading people not to be enslaved by private property is worthwhile, but it must be seen as part of a wider struggle. If all oppressive governments stopped imprisoning, torturing and killing people, this would not necessarily lead to 'true freedom'. It would create more physical freedom for some, even millions, of individuals, but it would not create human freedom, which demands 'the conquest of new, qualitatively different ways of being a man in order to achieve an ever more total and complete fulfilment of the individual in solidarity with all mankind' (ibid., pp. 32–3). The Western understanding of man cannot conceive of a new man. But we cannot even achieve the negative part of overcoming oppression unless we are at least open to this possibility, because to deny this possibility is to accept the values which underpin the present practice of oppression. Reformist activity, which is all that can follow from a moralistic concern about the facts of oppression, is not only inadequate but, if seen as the total solution, self-defeating and counter-productive. It is not surprising, therefore, that, as Gutierrez says when speaking of the dependence of some countries on others as one of the most profound causes of oppression, 'Attempts to bring about changes within the existing order have proved futile ... Only a radical break from the status quo, that is, a profound transformation of the private property system, access to the power of the exploited class, and a social revolution that would break this dependence would allow for the change to a new society' (ibid., p. 26).

Like Gutierrez, I believe, both as a Christian and as a socialist, that that is possible; the individualist believes that it is neither possible nor desirable. Believing in the possibility does not, of course, bring it about. But unless one believes in a *common* destiny for mankind which can be achieved, rather than individual salvation both in a religious and secular sense, there is no real reason for being concerned about other people at all, except perhaps that it makes you feel good. And it is easier to make yourself feel good by busying yourself with such obvious good works as trying to get people out of prison than it is, for example, by attacking the institution of private property.

I repeat that I am not decrying the need for and the importance of such works. I am saying, firstly, that an individualistic view of man provides an excuse for many people not to do even that much; and, secondly, that it cannot provide a basis for the achievement of even the limited efforts it may inspire. It can neither explain nor overcome oppression. The lack of success in ridding the world of oppression is not due to a lack of effort on the part of human rights campaigners, and it cannot be achieved by a multiplication of those efforts. The efforts are not ends in themselves; they must have an objective. If this objective is anything less than the creation of a totally new society, even the most well-intentioned efforts will be suborned into the service of the present one, as indeed they are. Witness Amnesty International's efforts in the Central African Empire, where its exposure of the murder of between fifty and a hundred children at least contributed to the downfall of 'Emperor' Bokassa, who was becoming notorious for the brutality of (and his personal participation in) his treatment of both political opponents and criminals. Jonathan Power, in his eulogy on Amnesty, *Against Oblivion*, describes this as 'one of Amnesty's greatest breakthroughs'. But breakthrough to what? To overcoming oppression, or to furthering French interests in Africa?

In May 1979 Amnesty issued a press release stating that it 'had received reliable reports that between fifty and a hundred children had been killed in prison. A witness said the bodies of sixty-two dead children had been buried by government officers during the night of 18 April alone.' The subsequent publicity led a Conference of French-speaking African heads of state, which was attended by President Giscard d'Estaing, to send a Commission of Inquiry to the Central African Empire. The Commission's report, which was published in August, confirmed Amnesty's findings. Meanwhile Bokassa had gone to Libya to seek assistance. 'During his absence,' Amnesty blandly reports, 'French troops arrived in Bagui and installed David Dacko as the new President.' There is no doubt that Bokassa was responsible for these and other killings and that he deserved to be exposed and deposed – at least. But the reporting of 'the facts' in isolation did not necessarily further the cause of overcoming oppression, unless one assumes that the French, being Western, knew best and that their influence was as benign as their motives were noble. That might have been the case; but neither Amnesty nor Power appears even to consider the possibility of the opposite.

'In the end,' says Power, 'not only did Amnesty reveal one of the most horrible events of the last decade; the disclosure also provoked the French government into sending in paratroopers to depose a tyrant who had become an embarrassment' (ibid., p. 49). But what is the relationship between these facts? It is significant that, according to Power, Amnesty's first intimation of the events came from its representative in Paris and that the accuracy of the reports was confirmed by Bokassa's ambassador in Paris. (I am not suggesting that there was any deliberate collusion between Amnesty and the French government, or that the French government did have ulterior motives; only that the latter is a possibility and that Amnesty's method of working provides the opportunity for its support being absorbed into the service of nefarious political ends.) Were the French 'provoked', or were they looking for an excuse? Did Bokassa become an embarrassment after the facts had been exposed, or was he one beforehand? Once the facts had been exposed by Amnesty and confirmed by the Commission of inquiry, who could object to French paratroopers going into a foreign state to depose a murderer of children? Nobody would be concerned about who was installed in his place, since he could surely not be worse than Bokassa. The French were therefore able to install whomsoever they wanted without any fear of protests being made.

Amnesty's failure to consider these questions is not simply a mark of political naïveté; it is the inevitable consequence of being concerned only with 'the facts' of oppression. Facts do not exist by themselves. It is not possible to separate, as Power does, the 'events' from 'the political relationship that creates the environment that spawns and nurtures such behaviour'. The 'facts' of oppression are part of the total reality of oppression, which can neither be explained nor changed in terms of an exclusive concern with individuals and isolated 'facts'.

If oppression is neither part of human nature nor a necessary consequence of particular individual qualities, it can only be explained by something supra-individual which all oppressors have in common. I am not about to launch into a theological dissertation, though I believe that theology is able to throw considerable light on the subject. As Miranda says, 'The most revolutionary historical thesis, in which, in contrast with all Western ideologies, the Bible and Marx coincide, is this: Sin and evil, which were later structured into an enslaving civilizing system, are not inherent to mankind and history; they began one day through a human work and can, therefore, be eliminated. The entire West had relegated this conviction to the archive of utopias' (*Marx and the Bible*, pp. 254–5).

This 'supra-individual' reality is not, as Miranda points out, a 'mythological personification', nor is it simply the state or government. Oppression is practised by states which are diametrically opposed to each other and by groups which do not constitute a state or a government. All that they have in common is that they are oppressive, and oppressive groups have existed since the dawn of civilization. Oppression pre-dates any existing ideology or governmental form of oppression, even capitalism and Western civilization, by several thousand years. The Old Testament, for example, is full of accounts of oppression and the struggle against it, while Marx asserts that 'the history of all hitherto existing society is the history of class struggles'. The various forms of oppression are particular manifestations of a larger reality. Neither the prevention of isolated instances of oppression nor even the overthrow of individual oppressive governments will overcome oppression.

The present manifestations of oppression owe their immediate origins, which may go back hundreds or even thousands of years, to the deliberate actions of some person or persons; to the desire of some people to dominate and exploit other people. The consequent practice and the inequalities and suffering which follow from it are then 'justified' by myths of inequality and difference and by whole philosophical systems. The practice of racism in Britain, for example, doubtless has its roots in the slave trade and in centuries of ill-treatment of black people. Over the years people come to believe that black people are inferior because they have always been treated as inferior; the conditions which created the myth are used to justify it. But that does not explain the need for creating the myth; it does not explain why some people chose to put their own individual liberty and prosperity before other people. It does not answer the question put by Robert Sobukwe, the late leader of the South African liberation group, the Pan African Congress. I trust readers will allow me a little personal reminiscence about this great man before I come to his question.

I once spent a couple of hours walking around Kimberley with him under the watchful and not noticeably friendly gaze of literally dozens of Security Police, who were standing in groups on every corner and patrolling the streets in cars. Sobukwe had not long been released from Robben Island, where he had been sent to serve a three-year sentence, which had been extended, by a special Act of Parliament each year, for a further six years. He was finally released and placed under house-arrest. The government refused him permission to leave the country, fearing no doubt that he was perhaps the only person, since Mandela was still on the Island, who could unite the liberation movement. Sobukwe was, therefore, no armchair theorist. He was a committed Christian and socialist, a devotee to some extent of Leopold Senghor, and the father figure of the Black Consciousness Movement. We were discussing the relationship between these factors in South African society. (I was actually going around South Africa meeting church and political leaders – mainly Blacks – to discuss the setting up of a working group on Black Consciousness, Socialism and Christianity. It never materialized because by the time I had finished my tour only two of the Blacks I had seen were not in prison; though the arrest of the others had not been occasioned, I trust, by my visit.) Sobukwe agreed that there could be no real change in South Africa without some form of socialism. But, he added, 'For us the main question is not about either the accumulation of wealth or the manner of its distribution. We ask, "Why wealth?"'

I do not think that even Marx's 'solution to the riddle of history' gives a satisfactory and intelligible answer to that question. The desire for wealth, more specifically for private ownership of wealth, is the proximate cause of the existing forms of oppression. But why do people have this desire? Capitalism provides the structures within which this desire can be fulfilled; but what caused the structures to be set up in the first place? I have not made a detailed study of Marx and I do not profess to have a clear understanding of much of the theoretical debate conducted by his followers. But on this point he does not seem even to answer his own questions. He establishes that private property is the necessary consequence of alienated labour and then asks: 'How is this estrangement rooted in the nature of human development?' He does not, however, seem to give an answer, and one can hardly assume that he meant to imply that it was 'natural'. This is not really a criticism of Marx, since he was primarily concerned with fighting against the current evils of capitalism. This he did with great moral fervour, but not as an 'irrational crusade'. He did ask the question, and presumably somewhere gave the answer to his own satisfaction. One explanation with which he was far from satisfied was the so-called 'Christian' one. 'These Christian principles,' he said, 'explain all the vile actions to which the oppressed are subjected by their oppressors either as just chastisement for original sin ... or as tests imposed on the elect by God in his wisdom.' There is no doubt that this was the explanation given by Christian teachers in Marx's time and by many before and since. It does not, however, explain the cause; nor is it Christian.

Many people have been influenced, and even anaesthetized, by a literal interpretation of the biblical account of 'the Fall', which says that everything was created perfectly by God but man – even one man – ruined it by sinning and, as a consequence, all men are prone to evil. It was doubtless this teaching which led Locke to postulate the existence of man enjoying perfect freedom in a state of nature. And it continues to exert an influence even on those who would not claim to be Christians; it has become part of the mythology of Western civilization and lends support to the view that at least man's propensity to oppress and to exploit is part of the natural order. But belief in the existence of a state of nature is not essential to Christian theology. This theology does not teach that all the evil in the world stems from the action of a single man in a particular historical time and place. It cannot teach that, because it would be impossible for a perfect man in a perfect environment to do wrong. Wrong is the consequence of man being faced with a good and an evil and choosing what is, or what he perceives to be, the evil. But in a perfect society there would be no evil and a perfect man would not be able mistakenly to perceive something good as an evil. The Christian doctrine of 'the Fall', therefore, cannot explain the historic origins of evil in the world. It is now generally agreed by biblical scholars that the Paradise described in the Book of Genesis refers to the *future* of man, not to his historic past. The teaching does, however, confirm that, whatever the precise manner of man's coming on to the scene, he did not enter into a perfectly ordered society. 'The Fall' shows that evil or disorder is even more 'original' than man; it becomes 'sin' when man accepts it. The Bible teaches that in sinning man acts *contrary* to his nature; far from being natural to man, it is precisely the fact that it is against his nature that makes the action 'sin' and not simply 'disorder'. The *natural* state of man is the perfection which is described as his future. The Bible does not explain how that state of affairs arose nor why men made the decisions they did. But it was only *possible* for them to choose wrongly because they were *not yet* perfect. In any event, even a literal interpretation of the Fall does not provide Christians with an excuse for accepting the status quo, as has been their wont, because Christianity also teaches that, whatever the nature and consequences of the Fall, Christ rectified them. Christianity believes in the 'redeemed nature', not in the 'fallen nature', of man. It does not believe that there is a separate Christian or theological explanation for the existence of historical events; it is the task of theology to give meaning to actual historical events.

'Primitive accumulation', according to Marx, 'plays in political economy about the same part as original sin in theology. Adam bit the apple and thereupon sin fell on the human race.' But Adam didn't 'bite the apple' and he could not have done so unless he lived in an imperfect society. Likewise, primitive accumulation could not have taken place in a perfect society; it cannot, therefore, explain the ultimate origin of all imperfections of society. Neither Marx nor a Christian could say that these arose simply because some people were bad. Neither the origin nor the present practice of oppression can be explained by the nastiness of some people. The sadism of the individual torturer does not explain how and why he is in a position to derive pleasure from the practice of his 'craft'. There might be psychological explanations for the particular methods that oppressors use; for the fact, for example, that torture has only been practised for the past few thousand years after man had survived for hundreds of thousands of years without it. But abnormalities, perversions or instinctual natural drives cannot be the ultimate source of unnatural actions.

Only man is capable of moral actions; the evil of oppression can, therefore, only be ascribed to man. But this does not make him responsible for the origin of oppression as a physical reality, or for the present totality of that reality. I do not see how there can be any *rational* answer to the ultimate

'Why?', because if man first appeared in a disordered society, as both the Bible and secular history suggest, there could be no rational explanation for that state of affairs, nor any moral responsibility for it, since by definition it was not the work of man. This does not take away the moral responsibility of man both for the beginning of oppression in history and for the present practice of it. Man did not *have* to continue living according to the law of the jungle. We could not, however, expect our primitive ancestors to foresee all the consequences of their actions, and we cannot attribute the moral blame for the vast, complex system of capitalism to their primitive accumulation. They were morally and humanly responsible only for deciding to accommodate themselves to the disorder rather than to change it. They accepted the disorder, which had been a stage of development reached in a pre-human context, as being natural for them; but it was not natural for human beings, whose nature is to continue the development until it reaches perfection. If it had been natural there would be no reason to blame them at all. But oppression in any form is no more natural to humans than swinging in trees is. What is natural to man is the ability to choose, not the exercise of choice in any particular way. Man acts on the world, but the world also acts on man. Man is, therefore, responsible for choosing to oppress and to exploit, but he could not have made that choice unless the conditions for oppression and exploitation were already present. This does not explain why, in a particular instance, an individual should choose evil rather than good; but every such action is a refusal to admit that it is possible for man to change. As far as oppression is concerned, it shows that to say it is ultimately part of the 'natural order of things' is to judge human beings by a prehistoric norm. Civilization has managed to systematize and codify the law of the jungle and to make that the summit of human achievement.

People are, and doubtless always have been, selfish, aggressive, acquisitive, greedy – all individual 'qualities' which are expressions of concern for oneself as opposed to concern for others or for the community as a whole; they are individualistic traits. If human nature is defined only in terms of what is, that is not only what man is – a selfish, aggressive creature – but it is all that he can be; after all, it's natural. But the fact that man *can* choose, and that it is this which distinguishes him from other species, shows that his ability to change, rather than his immobilization in a particular stage of evolution, is part of his nature. The fact that he is still selfish is only proof that he is not yet fully human. Conservatism and liberalism, which are based on Western individualism, are not only opposed to change; they have defined human nature in terms which preclude change. They might admit that some improvement is possible; that it is possible for man to move on at some later date; but they do not accept that the ability to move on is part of the *present* nature of man. But the *human* qualities of man cannot be defined simply in terms of what individuals are or appear to be, because the sum total of individuals who have existed and do exist do not constitute humanity.

'From the moment when men have awoken to an explicit consciousness of the evolution that carries them along, and begin to fix their eyes, as one man, on one same thing ahead of them,' says Teilhard de Chardin, 'by that very fact they must surely begin to love one another' (Segundo, op. cit.). And it is only then that they can. The arrival of that moment will be postponed for as long as Western individualism makes the opposite, the consciousness of our individualism and the concern for the destiny of the individual, its goal. An individual can only fulfil himself as a human being in solidarity with all other human beings. The attainment of universal respect for *human* rights on the basis of an individualistic philosophy is not only impossible for practical reasons – the scope and intensity of modern forms of oppression and the indifference of so many people; it is also self-contradictory. For the individualist there are no *human* rights, there are only individual rights, which can only be defined in terms of what is. And what is, for most people, is unfreedom and inequality – oppression. It is not possible to overcome oppression if the present individual 'qualities' which lead people to practise it are part of human nature. If man is, by nature, what he is, he simply cannot, by definition, be what he should be. But for the individualist there is no 'should be' for man; only for the individual. And that 'should be' for the individual cannot go beyond the 'natural' selfishness and aggressiveness of man.

Any campaigning for human rights which accepts this, even implicitly, is actually working against human freedom. This happens when, in Amnesty for example, people are concerned solely with obtaining the release from prison of an individual. This is not a question, as Amnesty says, of 'our freedom in defence of theirs'. Such an approach reinforces the assumption on which oppression itself is based. If our freedom and theirs are separate and if both are important, then the importance of our freedom can, and does provide an excuse for suppressing the freedom of others just as well as it can provide a reason for defending it. As we have seen, the importance of '*our*' freedom is used quite unashamedly by Hayek, for example, to justify the denial of equality – and consequently also of freedom – to others. If freedom can be divided and allocated to individuals, so can oppression. As a result, oppression will be attacked in a piecemeal, and necessarily ineffective way. If we recognized the indivisibility of freedom and the totality of oppression, we would have to acknowledge both that we are unfree and that we share in the oppression. To escape this we seek refuge in individualism; we are all right, as individuals; the oppressors are all wrong, as individuals.

Oppression did not burst upon the world in a fully fledged state; it grew. It grew from prehistoric roots and was planted in history by comparatively innocuous actions; innocuous compared, that is, both to the consequences that have followed from them and to the heinousness of a crime which could by itself completely disrupt the whole course of history. It then became structured into a system by the legalizing of these actions; law has more to do with oppression than it has with liberation. Selfishness, for example, became protected by law and ultimately entrenched as an unquestioned right. The system developed a momentum of its own; it became, and still is, something bigger than the sum total of the actions, for which people are responsible, which constitute it. While a person in a primitive society could indulge his selfishness or anger without doing, or even being able to do, a great deal of harm to others, in our present society the same degree of selfishness or anger can and does lead to the exploitation of thousands of people or even the death of millions. Man has created a monster which he cannot control but which, rather, controls him. This was not a discovery or 'theory' of Marx; as Miranda remarks, 'the totality and organicity of injustice structured into civilization was pointed out by Paul eighteen centuries before Marx'.

This does not, however, provide an excuse for present-day oppressors. They are responsible for their individual actions, but these actions also participate in the evilness of the larger reality, which in turn provides the opportunity for them to take place; they are responsible for what they do, but they are not responsible for being able to do it. Any evil, including oppression, does not come solely from man or solely from society, but from the interaction between the two. Human beings and the world, as Paulo Freire says, 'come together as unfinished products in a permanent relationship, in which human beings transform the world and undergo the effects of their transformation' (*Education for Critical Consciousness*, p. 147). Only an individualist philosophy sees man as completely responsible for his own actions and for his own actions alone; on the other hand, only a mechanistic interpretation of Marxism sees man as entirely the product of circumstances. Marx himself pointed out: 'The materialist theory that men are the product of circumstances and of education, and that, therefore, modified men are the product of different circumstances, and a different education, forgets that the circumstances are actually transformed by men and that the educator himself needs to be educated.' Oppressors could act otherwise, but they could not act as they do were it not for oppressive structures and the total reality of oppression. They cannot therefore be changed simply as individual people or governments.

I realize that I have only superficially, even simplistically, touched upon very profound questions. To go into them properly would require many volumes; to answer them fully would be beyond my – and I think anybody's – capabilities. Anyone who is concerned about overcoming oppression and not just with doing 'good works' must, however, face them; they are not of purely philosophical or anthropological interest. We can then at least rid ourselves of any hangover from the opiate of the 'natural order of things' and be convinced of the possibility of transforming the present disorder into a truly human order. Amnesty International appropriately chose hope as the theme for its twentieth anniversary year in 1981. But there is no basis for hope in past or present 'successes'. Hope can only be inspired by a vision of the future and by a realization that the future is already present: that man is not only what he is; he is what he will be and what he should be. The transformation of the former into the latter is a long and gradual process, but it is not a piecemeal one. It can neither be achieved in one fell swoop nor by actions which, leaving aside all political and social considerations, are concerned solely with man as an individual. I am not suggesting that we should do nothing until we have found the perfect method for doing everything, but that we cannot do anything unless we have the perfect as our objective. To be satisfied with less is literally an insult to humanity.

History is not made by debating the relationship between individual liberty and equality or between the individual and the state. It is made by resolving the conflict between indivisible human freedom and equality on the one hand, and organic, not just organized, oppression on the other. We are not faced with the dilemma of having to choose between a free but unequal society and an equal but unfree one, unless we accept the validity and immutability of the Western individualistic view of man. In that case the conflict is irresolvable and the only question is: How great a price must some people pay for the individual freedom of others? But there is no conflict between human freedom and human equality. In a society which is based on a Western view of man there is not – nor can there be – either freedom or equality in a human sense. It is the capitalist system, which is based on this view, that essentially and necessarily dehumanizes man, since it separates and contrasts liberty and equality, and reduces man to 'economic man'. For the socialist, as Marx said, man's greatest wealth is other people: 'Poverty is the passive bond which causes the human being to experience the need of the greatest wealth – the *other* human being.' Whereas, for the capitalist, man's wealth is the greater the more he can take from other people.

We cannot, however, compare socialist theory with capitalist practice; in practice, socialist states have not only been judged and found wanting, according to Western norms, but those in power have tended to retain an allegiance to capitalist values, at least for themselves. The fact that there is not yet a society where equality and freedom for all are more important than the wealth of some is no proof that there cannot be one. It only confirms the fact that man and society are both 'unfinished products'. But if, because of the nature of man, there cannot be one, we have no reason to complain about the present state of affairs anywhere nor to blame anyone for it: nor do we have any grounds for hoping for an improvement. The theory of the separability of equality and freedom, and of their necessarily being in conflict, 'justifies' the steps which have been taken to establish the present forms of oppression in both capitalist and socialist countries.

CHAPTER 6

CAPITALISM AND OPPRESSION

Even its own apologists agree that some degree of inequality is inevitable, necessary and acceptable in a capitalist system. Equality, they argue, can only be imposed at the cost of limiting the individual's freedom to be different, to be competitive and to receive the material rewards of his efforts. It is admitted that it is only the few who need to be free of any restriction on their individual liberty. 'It is certainly more important,' says Hayek, 'that anything can be tried by somebody than that all can do the same things' (*The Constitution of Liberty*, p. 32). It is only the few who have the skill and knowledge to ensure progress in the arts, science, politics and every other aspect of life. We do not know who the few are, so we must accord individual liberty to all; the few will then be free to act for the benefit of the whole of society. It is only because of its respect for individual liberty, they say, that the West has made so much progress. The consequent inequality is nothing compared to the oppression of individuals which necessarily takes place in socialist countries. When oppression is present on a vast scale, both in terms of denial of freedom and equality (as in South Africa and in most Latin American countries), this is ascribed to racism or to the fact that they have military and not Western democratic governments.

The fact that there is inequality even in the most developed capitalist countries does not need any proof. It is not surprising that in Britain, for instance, the *per capita* income of the 'top' 20 per cent of the population is about five times that of the 'bottom' 50 per cent. But there is no freedom either, not even for the few. An illusion of freedom is created in order to perpetuate the inequality. People are free, we are told, of any coercion by other *people*; any limitations which exist are either the result of impersonal forces or arise from arrangements which are freely entered into. The capitalist himself is not free. He has to obey the forces of the market. But, as Richard Turner says,

> the market is not a force of nature. It is *other people* going about their
> business. It is other people limiting what I can do. When there is a slump

and a rise in unemployment, the limitations being placed on people thereby are a result of investment decisions and other commercial decisions made by other people. When I send my apples to market and find there is a glut, it is because other people have been planting, growing, picking and packing too many apples for the needs of yet other people, who will not buy any more apples because they have had enough. The force of the market is ... a hidden social force. It is other people telling me what to do. In any society I have to adjust what I am doing to fit in with what other people are doing, and vice versa. To call a society in which I am told what to do, indirectly and invisibly, a 'free society', whilst calling a society in which the limitations operate directly an 'unfree society' is just nonsense (*The Eye of the Needle*, p. 48).

The glut could be avoided with a little planning, but that would interfere with the individual's freedom, which has been made into an inviolable principle precisely in order to leave the capitalist 'free' to manipulate the forces of the market.

The workers are not free, not only because they are victims of this manipulation, but also because they are further shackled by a lack of information and by the necessity of earning a living. A person's freedom to choose is determined by the information available. Anybody who has serviced a committee knows that, if you present the decision-makers only with information which supports the wisdom of the decision you want and only that which shows the futility of any other, you do in fact take the decision for them. In a capitalist society this is done on a vast scale through control of the education system and of the media. People cannot be free to choose an alternative if it is never presented to them. They are also not free – in any meaningful sense of the word – to choose to allow not only themselves but also their dependants to starve, which is the only alternative to accepting a wage. Even the 'freedom' of collective bargaining in setting wages is limited since there is not free collective bargaining in setting prices and, since those who pay the wages also set the prices, any increase in the former is offset by an increase in the latter. Workers are forced ultimately to accept the wages offered and by so doing are forced to accept their inferior status in the whole system, because they are forced to agree that they are worth less than some others. Their worth as people is measured by their monetary worth as workers; consequently they are less entitled to other rights or freedoms which belong to people.

The inequality and the unfreedom perpetuate each other. The denial of freedom, which is inherent in the capitalist myth that prices are set not by them but by market forces, prevents the workers from having any power to organize as consumers and hence to gain any real increase in their share of the national income. There is no point in having more money if it will not buy more things. More money for the workers also means more money for the capitalists, but their respective, unequal shares of the goods and services that constitute the national income remain much the same. The workers' share would, of course, become progressively less if they did not have the power to organize as workers; but this power alone cannot achieve equality and, consequently, freedom.

It is the exercise of this power by the workers in the Western capitalist countries which has prevented the steady erosion of their freedom and equality and has even achieved a slight increase in their share of the income. Further, because of the diversified nature of capitalism in these countries, more people partake in the total capitalist share. Thus in Britain there has over the past fifteen years or so been a significant redistribution of income within the 'top' 30 per cent of the population. But the share of the bottom 30 per cent has only fractionally increased. (The others inhabit the famous 'middle ground' which 'wet' Tories, the Social Democratic Party and the right wing of the Labour Party are all trying to occupy.) The disparity is not as great as it might have been, not only because of the organized efforts of the workers themselves, but also because Western capitalism is based on the gross exploitation of the material resources and of the people of its former colonies. And in the history of colonialism there is no evidence that Western capitalists were loath to resort to the most brutal forms of oppression. This exploitation is responsible both for creating the conditions for capitalism to flourish in the West without intense political repression, and for causing the instability which is the proximate cause of much of the repression in Africa. Greg Lanning, in his mammoth work on the role of the mining companies in undermining Africa politically, economically and socially, comments:

> In the course of the violent and turbulent pursuit of profits over the last hundred years, the companies have changed the face of Africa. When economic muscle and financial manipulation proved insufficient to secure 'stability' and a favourable investment climate, the companies detonated *coups d'état*, bankrolled armies, organized wars, launched invasions, hired mercenaries, de-stabilized governments, started political parties, corrupted politicians and uprooted millions of African peasants (Lanning and Mueller, *Africa Undermined*, p. 422).

The capitalists' preoccupation with individual liberty has nothing to do with a desire to promote artistic or scientific progress. They are prepared not only to allow, but positively to encourage, individuals to express their freedom in other ways in order to distract attention from the denial of freedom which is inherent in their system. Even workers are able to have some share in these other freedoms, but since they have already been forced to sell their souls, they cannot derive any really human benefit from them. In the West this process has been institutionalized; in other capitalist countries it is still left to individuals. But for Harry Oppenheimer, for example, the couple of million pounds a year that he spends on African 'advancement' is a small price, less than 1 per cent of profits, to pay for the perpetuation of the system.

It might be argued that, even allowing that in addition to inequality there is less than perfect freedom in Western capitalist society, it cannot be called oppressive in anything but a metaphorical sense. The solution to the problem of oppression, therefore, is to minimize the degree of inequality by the extension of Western capitalism. Apart from any other considerations, this would simply not be possible because of the demands that the Western form of capitalism has made on natural resources; there would not be enough to go round. 'What has happened,' says Richard Lowenthal,

> is that, under the impulse of the profit motive, the forces of destruction have grown along with the forces of production – not only in the familiar sense of the increasing destructiveness of modern weapons, but of the destructive impact of modern industrial technology on the environment and the natural resources until they now threaten to outpace the latter. It looks as if the acceleration of technical progress under the profit system is tending to destroy its own material foundation (Kolakowski and Hampshire (ed.), *The Socialist Idea*, p. 235).

Further, it is at least disputable whether even the intensity of oppression in such societies is less than it is in socialist countries.

Socialist states are rightly considered oppressive because among other things, they imprison dissidents and people who want to leave the country. But in Britain, for example, we detain without trial, sometimes for a year or more, people who want to come into the country. And in proportion to the respective populations there are several hundred times more people unemployed in Britain than there are political prisoners in the Soviet Union, where there is virtually no unemployment. Imprisoning one person is considered more oppressive than making several hundred unemployed. On an individual level unemployment can be worse than imprisonment. I personally found unemployment in Britain a more degrading and dehumanizing experience than house-arrest in South Africa. (I also find the British police more intimidating than their South African counterparts.) By taking the trouble of putting me under house-arrest, the South African government at least recognized me as a person. The people at the Labour Exchange didn't. Not only was I a nobody, but I was a moronic nobody who had to be given instructions three times in words of one syllable and then asked to repeat them. And this even though I was a privileged unemployed person just as I was a privileged house-arrested person; the two experiences are, therefore, directly comparable. In Western society people are defined in terms of what they do; if they do nothing they are nothing. Political prisoners do not commit suicide; unemployed people do – not only because they have nothing, but because they are made to feel they *are* nothing. A political prisoner's life has meaning, an unemployed person's hasn't. It is not possible to compare and contrast economic deprivation with denial of political freedom, but there is a common standard of humanity. And, according to that standard, I do not believe that being confined to a psychiatric prison hospital for political reasons is any worse than being driven to commit suicide by being unemployed for economic reasons. For the victims the effect on their humanity is much the same. It is only those who are responsible for either who, to further their own political *and* economic interests, argue their relative importance in theory.

The Western democracies do not rely only on fostering the illusion of freedom and on practising institutionalized economic oppression in order to preserve the status quo; they also resort to overt political repression. Market forces, impersonal though they may be considered to be, need 'law and order' in order to operate smoothly. Any threats to 'law and order' must, therefore, be suppressed in the same way as deviationists are suppressed in socialist countries. The former are given a 'short, sharp shock' if they riot on the streets; the latter are given electric shocks. Law and order is maintained in Northern Ireland not only by military means but also by emergency legislation which, according to Amnesty International, virtually nullified the power of the courts over the arrest and detention of suspects. A judgement by Lord Chief Justice Lowry in June 1980

rejected any judicial responsibility to provide the remedy of habeas corpus even against 'an unacceptable but ostensibly lawful exercise of the powers of arrest' – such as repeated arrest and detention by the police of the same individual on the same suspicion, without bringing charges. The court had no power to inquire into the reasonableness of the arrest, he said, a remedy should be provided by the executive. There was therefore no effective remedy against arbitrary use of the emergency powers of arrest and detention by the police – contrary to international law (AI Annual Report, 1981, p. 338).

This applies whether or not people have used violence. Even those who have used violence, however, may still be political prisoners. In fact, if terrorism is defined as the use of violence for political ends, anybody arrested under the Prevention of Terrorism Act is by definition a political prisoner. The powers given by that Act are not used only in respect of 'terrorists': according to Amnesty's reports 'they have allegedly' [even Bokassa only 'allegedly' killed the children] 'been used to detain people holding minority political opinions, or regarded as supporters of the aims (though not necessarily the means) of violent political groups'. The exercise of such powers necessarily leads to individual horror stories such as that of Stephen Paul McCaul, who (in December 1971) was found guilty, on the basis of his own oral and written statements, of hijacking buses and various other offences. He was fifteen years old at the time, but

> he was mentally retarded, attended a special school and could neither read nor write, although he could write his name. Although the police were aware of these facts he was held incommunicado and questioned, without his parents or a lawyer or other third party present, in breach of regulations. According to uncontroverted psychiatric evidence the boy had a mental age of seven and was highly suggestible. The psychiatrist said he could not accept that Stephen McCaul could have dictated the statement alleged to have been made by him (ibid.).

He was nevertheless sentenced to three years' detention in a Young Offenders Centre. The judgement was upheld on appeal, but he was released in early 1981.

There are, of course, many similar instances, not only in Northern Ireland. Concern for 'law and order' is just as much part of a political ideology as is the demand for conformity with the Party line. Threats to law and order will, obviously, more often take the form of 'violence' – as defined by the upholders of law and order – than threats to ideological purity, but there is no reason for considering the former criminal and the latter political, though they might well both be wrong in particular instances.

Violence as a threat to the status quo is a crime, but so, in many Western countries, is the rejection of violence as a means of defending it – as conscientious objectors in many European countries have found. In Greece, for example, Amnesty was in 1981 working for the release of seventy-five imprisoned conscientious objectors. They were all Jehovah's Witnesses who refused any form of military service. 'Consequently they were tried for disobedience by a court martial and were usually sentenced to four and a half years' imprisonment, plus deprivation of civil rights for five years' (ibid., p. 300). There are numerous other examples of the imprisonment of people for politically motivated actions, and of their being ill-treated. An Amnesty report on prison conditions in West Germany, published in May 1980, found that the strict isolation imposed on some prisoners 'could seriously affect their physical and mental health, and had done so in a number of cases' (ibid., p. 280). This conclusion 'has never been disputed by the authorities, and has been explicitly confirmed by the courts' (ibid.). Amnesty continued to be concerned about the practice in 1981.

American capitalism, which was founded on the gross exploitation of its own indigenous people and of Latin America, and which continues to export a major part of its inequality, still 'needs' political repression at home as well as in El Salvador, Guatemala, Chile and elsewhere. Economic coercion alone is not enough to ensure that Blacks and American Indians remain unequal. If America is prepared to overthrow governments to protect its interests (these are essentially economic interests, since the only reason for wanting a political sphere of influence opposed to communist influence is to defend the present capitalist system), it is not surprising that they are prepared to 'neutralize' individuals. The FBI is a particularly well-known tool of oppression for this purpose, as is illustrated in an Amnesty Report, 'Proposal for a commission of inquiry into the effects of domestic intelligence activities on criminal trials in the United States of America'. Through its Counter Intelligence Program 'the arsenal of techniques used against foreign espionage agents was transferred to domestic enemies'. 'The result,' the Report continues, 'was that the right of US citizens to engage in free and open discussion and to associate with anyone they choose was jeopardized and "chilled" ... Undoubtedly there is a clear distinction between the "chilling" of constitutional rights and the imprisonment of individuals on political grounds.' It is only a difference of degree, and the difference is not necessarily very great unless one accepts Amnesty's assumption that imprisonment is the worst of all possible fates. But that is only true of people who consider their own individual freedom to be the most important consideration. One of the objects of the Program was to 'prevent the rise of a messiah who could unify and electrify the militant nationalist movement ... Martin Luther King, Stokely Carmichael, and Elijah Muhammed all aspire to this position'. The need for a messiah only arises when there is a group which is being systematically persecuted, not where there are disparate individuals with their own personal grievances. The Program was, therefore, more than an attack on the rights of a few individuals. As the 'Church Report' noted, 'key activists were not chosen because they were suspected of having committed or planning to commit any specific federal crime'.

The Amnesty Report deals with cases of the imprisonment of Blacks and members of the American Indian Movement and in particular with those of Elmer Pratt, a former leader of the Black Panther Party, and of Richard Marshall, a member of the American Indian Movement, both of whom were serving life sentences for murder as a result, they claimed, of being framed. 'The main difference between the two cases,' says the Report, 'is that Elmer Pratt was "targeted for neutralization" before his arrest while Richard Marshall was "targeted for investigation" the day after.' Whether either or both were in fact guilty is not Amnesty's point nor mine; nor am I interested in all the legal technicalities or in the precise role which the FBI and its informants play in particular trials, though the Report does indeed raise serious questions about this. Amnesty's main concern is that FBI misconduct and harassment prejudiced the right of these two and others to a fair trial. But 'it is not the number of cases discussed in this report that is important but the apparent relationship between domestic intelligence activity and the criminal justice system. Since misconduct by a law enforcement agency may at first sight appear to be an isolated incident, it is important to decide whether or not it is, in fact, part of a pattern' (p. 8). Hence the proposal for a Commission of Inquiry.

There are wider implications than the relationship between the FBI and the criminal justice system. The two cases are more than examples even of a 'pattern' of unfair trials; they are part of a pattern of internal political repression, which is just as cold, calculated and brutal as that engaged in by BOSS or the KGB. The Church Committee, which is quoted in the Report, after examining the FBI's tactics for fostering violence, concluded: 'The chief investigative branch of the Federal government, which was charged by law with investigating crimes and preventing criminal conduct, itself engaged in lawless tactics and responded to deep-seated social problems by fermenting violence and unrest.' The problems are 'deep-seated' in the essentially unequal system. As an example of the tactics, the Committee reported that

in Southern California, the FBI launched a covert effort to 'create further dissension in the ranks of the BPP' (Black Panther Party). This effort included mailing anonymous letters and caricatures to BPP members, ridiculing the local and national BPP leadership for the express purpose of exacerbating an existing 'gang war' between the BPP and an organization called the United Slaves (US). The 'gang war' resulted in the killing of four BPP members by members of US and in numerous beatings and shootings. Although individual incidents in this dispute cannot be directly traced to efforts by the FBI, FBI officials were clearly aware of the violent nature of the dispute, engaged in actions that they hoped would prolong and intensify the dispute, and proudly claimed credit for violent clashes between the rival factions which, in the words of one FBI official, resulted in 'shootings, beatings and a high degree of unrest'.

The South African security forces used the same tactics when they incited the migrant workers to attack the students during the Soweto riots.

The point of these few examples is not to show that there is at present the same amount of oppression in Western capitalist countries as there is in socialist countries, though that might well be the case. It is certainly the case that there is not as much overt and brutal political oppression, nor as great a degree of inequality as there is in other capitalist countries.

Western capitalists would argue that the gross inequality and the severe political repression in such countries are due to the fact that they have not yet developed Western democratic structures. Those structures have not prevented Western democracies being essentially oppressive, and being increasingly so when they are threatened. The one thing that is common to all capitalist systems is that the means of production are owned by a small section of the society. This means either that the rest of the population is forced into the wage-labour system, which necessarily causes economic coercion and a denial of freedom, and occasions political repression if there is any threat to the whole system; or that a class of landless peasants, with only the freedom to starve, is created. It is the particular form that capitalism takes in different countries, rather than the political structures, which determines the degree of oppression which is 'needed' for its development. The political structures are the means of preserving the economic system.

The sheer physical brutality of some forms of oppression cannot be ascribed to any natural or racial characteristics of those responsible. People of all colours, tribes and creeds have all shown themselves to be capable of the inhuman treatment of their fellow man. Amin's atrocities were no more due to his 'primitive' African-ness than Hitler's were to his 'advanced' Arian-ness. We cannot claim that the civilized nature of our Western society would prevent the sort of torture that is practised in Argentina or the shooting of innocent people that happens in places like El Salvador. The fact that they are 'hot-blooded Latins' has no more to do with the nature of their oppressive practices than it has with their sexual ones; at the very most that could only have some bearing on the techniques used. We, too, have done it and we can hardly say that we have evolved beyond that point; a couple of hundred years in the history of human evolution is but a moment. The West still kills and tortures people, but it generally does it more clinically and, if possible, at a distance. The Anglo-Saxon antipathy towards physical contact extends from embracing to killing and torturing. But there is no moral difference between killing and torturing people by dropping bombs or napalm on them and shooting or torturing them individually; for the victims there is no difference at all. There is no reason for assuming that, if 'necessary', Western democratic countries would not use the same means as their capitalist counterparts in South Africa or in Guatemala; they might, however, try to avoid literally getting blood on their hands. There is, of course, plenty of evidence of the upholders of 'law and order' in Britain, for example, not being averse even to that. Particular instances of brutality are the inevitable consequence of the institutionalization of inequality and consequent 'inferiority' in capitalist society. It is Blacks and working-class people who are the worst victims in Britain; Whites are not as badly tortured in South Africa as Blacks are. Even in Guatemala, where people of 'higher social and economic status' are suspected of 'subversive' activity, 'the discretionary powers of security service agents do not appear to be un-restricted ... the system appears to function hierarchically with the official level at which a decision may be taken corresponding to the status of the subject' (Amnesty Report on Guatemala, p. 6). It is not so much who does it as to whom it is being done that determines the degree of brutality.

It is, however, *economic* coercion which is essential to capitalism; some people have to be forced to work for wages otherwise there would be no profits. The degree of coercion does not depend only on the greed of the individual capitalist; it also depends on the nature of the enterprise and the exploitability of the workers. South Africa provides the best-documented example of extreme economic coercion and intense political repression, and possibly the most thoroughly analysed one from the point of view of the relationship between this oppression and capitalism. There is no need for me to expand on the descriptive part. South African capitalists are no greedier, and not noticeably richer than British capitalists. In the early days of South African capitalism, with the establishment of the gold- and diamond-mining industries, a greater amount of coercion was 'needed' in order to obtain the same amount of profit as could have been obtained in other forms of capitalist enterprise.

It would take a whole book to examine the growth and patterns of South African capitalism and its relationship to oppression. Several such books have indeed been written and I have written on it myself. Simply by way of example and with gross over-simplification, however, it can be said that if gold and diamonds had been nearer the surface there would at least be less oppression in South Africa today. Because of the difficulties in mining, a vast amount of labour was needed; the enterprise would not therefore have been worthwhile in capitalist terms unless this could be obtained cheaply – which meant extremely cheaply as far as each individual was concerned. The Whites could not be coerced into working for the low wage offered, because they could at least ensure their survival by other means. Africans were vulnerable to such coercion. They were living by subsistence farming and had little need for money. This need was created, however, by the imposition of a hut-tax. They were therefore forced to work for money at the only places available: the mines. They also had to be prepared to work even if they only received enough money to pay the hut-tax. They were thus exploited not only as workers, but as black workers, since, for political reasons (they had no votes) and economic reasons (they were subsistence farmers), 'black' was synonymous with 'exploited'. But just as any workers being forced into the wage-system are forced to accept an inferior status in the whole system, so these were forced to accept such status as *black* workers.

It is on such a free choice of a labour contract that the present systematic oppression in South Africa is based; it stems from the 'needs' of capitalism. Capitalism has developed; and so has oppression. The development, with the assistance of foreign investment, of capital-intensive forms of agriculture and manufacturing industries has, among other things, created a vast pool of unemployed workers (at least 25 per cent of the total African workforce). This serves both to keep the wages of the employed workers down and, since 25 per cent are getting nothing, increases the overall gap between capitalists and workers. The reluctance of the South African government to allow workers to organize effectively is, therefore, understandable in capitalist terms.

Economic coercion is not enough – not even, as we have indicated, in Western democracies; political repression is also 'needed' if there is any threat to the whole system. In the South African context, when land was the only source of wealth and Blacks had been physically subjugated into working it for them, the only threat was that they might wander off; repression, therefore, took the form of 'anti-vagrancy' laws. When large numbers of Africans were forced to go to the cities to meet the needs of capitalism, their presence there and the possibility of their organizing constituted a political threat, so more complex and more repressive controls were introduced; influx control, the Pass Laws, 'resettlement'. Despite this, Blacks did organize, so even more repressive measures were introduced to deal with political and trade union 'agitators': the Suppression of Communism Act, under which the African National Congress and the Pan African Congress were banned; the Terrorism Act; the Internal Security Act, and dozens of others. As capitalism develops the economic gap widens, and as resentment and political awareness increase so does political repression. Both the inequality and the repression make complete sense and are necessary – in capitalist terms. They result from following fundamentally the same path as Western capitalism (which, of course, is also partly responsible for the particular way in which South African capitalism has developed). South African capitalism has not been able to export part of the problem.

Capitalists, including South African ones, would prefer to rely simply on economic coercion to ensure they receive their share of the national wealth and income; after all, political repression is an expensive business. Liberal commentators often point out how financially wasteful the whole repressive machinery of apartheid is, but in capitalist terms it is not wasteful; it is expensive, but it is the only way of holding on to their share. The alternatives are to share or to oppress, and oppression costs less than they would lose by sharing with the total black population.

Elsewhere in Africa and in other parts of the world the colonizers were able to avoid imposing such a totally repressive system by co-opting a sizeable section of the indigenous population into the capitalist sytem. This did not happen in South Africa because from the beginning those who were exploitable were seen as Blacks, rather than as workers – partly for the reasons already given and partly as a rationalization of their extreme exploitation. Any subsequent political threat has been seen as coming from Blacks as Blacks; *all* Blacks, therefore, have to be repressed. Attempts are now being made to incorporate a few Blacks into the system, by the creation either of a small urban middle class (the 'liberal' capitalists' solution) or of a bureaucratic middle class in the 'homelands' (the Nationalists' solution). Neither of these can put an end to either the repression or the inequality – no capitalist solution can, for both political and economic reasons. Politically, too many Blacks are aware that their oppression has been caused by capitalism for a large enough number of them to be bought off by it; moreover, the Nationalists are limited politically because the majority of their constituents still perceive *all* Blacks as a threat, even though the leaders themselves are aware that this is part of the racist myth.

More importantly, for the point I am making here, is that the present oppressive system is not only the result of the particular way capitalism has developed, it is still 'necessary' to protect the interests of both international and South African capitalism. The history of and the present relationship between the two are very complex, but there are some obvious reasons for apartheid being in both their interests. Foreign capitalists have thousands of millions of pounds invested in South Africa, because they receive a higher return on it. They need a stable form of society. They cannot achieve this by giving Blacks a fair share – or even an equal share with white workers – because this would negate the very purpose of their being there. They cannot take their investments and put them elsewhere even if they were prepared to accept a lower return, because much of their investment is in the form of buildings and machinery. They have to stay; they cannot 'afford' to give Blacks an appreciably larger share in the income, and they need stability. Blacks, on the other hand, increasingly resent this state of affairs and resort to strikes, rioting and political activity. How else can stability be maintained than through political repression? And what more efficient form of society is there than the present one? Apartheid is as necessary to capitalism in South Africa as 'law and order' is to capitalism in the West. It involves a greater *degree* of repression because the inequality started from a more extreme base and because *all* Blacks – 70 per cent of the population – are seen as a threat.

It might be argued that, since so much of the capitalists' wealth is in the form of immovable assets, it would be in their interest to increase the Blacks' share of the income even if this took up most of their profits, because it would at least ensure that there would not be a violent revolution in which they would lose everything. Firstly, they no doubt realize that they will probably lose most, if not all, of such assets anyway when Blacks assume political power whether by violent or non-violent means, because they will implement some form of socialist system. It is, therefore, still in their capitalist interests to make as much as they can while they can – that is, for as long as an oppressive system can postpone political change and maintain inequality. Secondly, there is a large and increasing number of the black population who *cannot* be incorporated into the capitalist system. There are the people who have been 'marginalized', primarily as a result of the particular form South African capitalism has taken in recent years. Its emphasis on capital-intensive industry and methods of agriculture has not only created unemployment; it has also created the 'marginalized' people who have been dispossessed of their land (or the use of 'white' land in return for labour), and who are not needed either as part of the workforce or even as part of the reserve army of labour. The re-integration of these people into the economy would demand the creation of labour-intensive methods instead of the capital-intensive ones. That would involve disposing of millions of pounds worth of high-technology equipment, which would not make sense in capitalist terms. It does make sense in capitalist terms to dispose of the people. They are not rounded up and shot; they are dumped in the 'homelands' discreetly and left to die there – a form of genocide for which the progress of capitalism, which is by no means the preserve of Afrikaner racists or even exclusively of South Africans, is directly to blame.

This is part of the price of individual freedom in the capitalist sense. The capitalist must be free to make progress, and the latest technology from Europe or America is obviously progress. It is 'progress', the capitalists would say, not themselves, which is responsible for the unfortunate side-effects; some price always has to be paid for progress; the motor car is progress and that is responsible for more deaths than occur in the dumping grounds. The justification for motor cars, if they can be justified, is that more people benefit from them than are harmed by them. That cannot be said of capitalist progress in South Africa, or indeed anywhere. Neither South African capitalists nor the government can, in capitalist terms, be blamed for even the most intense forms of oppressions because, like the lesser forms of oppression in any capitalist system, they are simply due to impersonal forces which are set in motion by the exercise of individual liberty in the cause of progress. They cannot change without ceasing to be capitalists. Hardline capitalist governments are muted in their criticism of South Africa, if not totally silent, because they recognize a kindred spirit; more liberal and even some socialist ones are loud in their criticisms, but are confused by the racial component.

Capitalism, therefore, not only essentially leads to some form of oppression; because of the inherent inequality in the system and the consequent loss of freedom, it also directly leads to oppression in the most extreme forms. The aim is the same, whatever the form of oppression; it is only the means which are determined by particular historical, social and economic conditions. South Africa is the clearest example of this, although I must admit that it did not become clear to me until I stopped banging my head against the brick wall erected by the racial ideology and recognized the futility of trying to persuade white South Africans to see the error of their ways: as capitalists, they are not in error. Any form of capitalism would, in that context, 'have' to be severely oppressive; the present form, due largely to its relationship with international capitalism, is most severely oppressive.

There are, however, numerous other examples: one could take virtually any country in Latin America. There, too, political repression as an alternative to distribution of wealth is in the interests of both national and international capitalism. Janet Townsend points out that 'effective democracy over large areas of Latin America would present a serious threat to workers, investors, multi-national corporations and financial corporations in Western Europe, North America and Japan' (see Dowrick (ed.), *Human Rights: Problems, Perspectives and Texts*, p. 124).

I have not personally studied any of these countries in the depth necessary to identify the precise form of capitalism which has led to oppression in each case. Some general points can be made from an appraisal of the information, published by Amnesty and by Jonathan Power, about Guatemala. They illustrate, in fact, the whole point of this book: the need to analyse and to gain an understanding of 'the facts'. They both give graphic descriptions of what is, and has been, happening in Guatemala; they deal with who gets killed, how they get killed and who kills them; they *assume*, however, a cause which does not provide an explanation. Power suggests that this is not important. He concludes his account: 'This may or may not be an accurate reading of the political situation. Whichever is the case, Amnesty will keep battering away at the excesses of Guatemala.' It is not only unreasonable, it is also highly irresponsible to 'batter away' when you do not know whether you are reading the situation correctly; Power himself points out that 'the killings have escalated since Amnesty sent a mission to Guatemala in 1979. Francisco Villagran (a former Vice-President now in exile), for one, feels that Amnesty's pressure in the short run might have been counter-productive ... Yet over the long run Amnesty may have been more effective than Carter' (op. cit., pp. 96–7). The justification for Amnesty's involvement is that it gives an enormous psychological boost to Guatemalan exiles. But it could do this without assuming *any* explanation if it restricted itself to its humanitarian aim of relieving suffering; it does not *have* to assume an essentially pro-capitalist one.

The explanation, which is stated in Power's work and implied by Amnesty, is that 'the will to change course does not seem to exist. Rule by violence has become embedded in the fabric of the Guatemalan government' (ibid., p. 96). The change which Power envisages as a possibility is one to a more conventional capitalist system: 'Diplomats and many dissidents agree that if the government-inspired violence were brought to a halt, if fair elections were allowed and the moderate left and centre "allowed room to breathe", if the Indians were protected from land grabs and given effective agricultural and medical aid, the guerillas would soon be isolated, enough

[sic] of their objectives achieved' (ibid.). The sum total of the arguments in the two quotations given is: If there was not severe oppression, severe oppression would not exist. But severe oppression does exist because it is embedded in society.

The severity of oppression in Guatemala cannot be doubted; Power considers that 'Guatemala has the worst human rights record of any Latin American country'; Amnesty and Power, however, seem more interested in playing detectives than in determining how violence has become embedded and how it can be eradicated. For example, Amnesty's Report contains information (which Power went to a great deal of trouble to verify), 'which shows how the selection of targets for detention and murder, and the deployment of official forces for extra-legal operations, can be pinpointed to secret offices in an annex of Guatemala's National Palace, under the direct control of the President of the Republic'. Amnesty's interviews with a peasant, who was thought to be the sole survivor of political imprisonment in Guatemala in 1980, and also with a conscript, are concerned only with isolated 'facts'. The questioning, in fact, becomes almost prurient: 'What torture did you see them inflict on the others? ... How did they torture you? ... Had they tortured this boy? ... Beaten him? ... Was electrical apparatus also used? ... You saw it? ... How did you feel then?' It is doubtless necessary to know such facts, but that is not all we need to know.

The 'selection of targets', for example, is more important and more revealing than the pinpointing of the actual room (sorry, *annex*) in which the decisions are taken. Amnesty's Report on this question is contradictory. It states that, while leaders of public opinion are detained and murdered, 'the vast majority of the victims of such violent action by the authorities' forces had little or no social status; they came from the urban poor and the peasantry and their personal political activities were either insignificant or wholly imagined by their captors' (p. 6). If that were the case there could be no effective political remedy and it would make no sense in capitalist terms. On the same page the Report gives what is more likely to be the true account:

At first glance most of the victims of political repression in Guatemala appear to have been singled out indiscriminately from among the poor; but the secret detentions, 'disappearances' and killings are not entirely random; they follow denunciations by neighbours, employers or local security officials, and the evidence available to Amnesty International reveals *a pattern of selective and considered, official* action. By far the majority of the victims were chosen after they had become associated – or were thought to be associated – with social, religious, community or labour organizations, or after they had been in contact with organizers of national political parties. In other words, Amnesty International's evidence is that the targets for extreme governmental violence tend to be selected from grassroots organizations outside official control.

That does make sense in capitalist terms. And it cannot be changed by appeals to their better nature; their nature has nothing to do with it, it is the nature of the capitalist system. Power confirms the latter account, albeit in a somewhat patronizing way, with a reference to 'simple peasant folk, [but] who have shown some initiative' (op. cit., p. 88).

Throughout Latin America, thanks in large part to the work of Paulo Freire, opposition groups have become aware of the supreme importance of grassroots organizations in the struggle against inequality and political repression. Capitalist governments are right to see them as a threat to the established system. To refer to these people as simple peasants whose political activities are insignificant is not only patronizing and offensive, it betrays a total failure to understand the problem. Necessary as it is to provide information about atrocities, a preoccupation with the gruesome details and a consideration of these in isolation prevents people from understanding what is really happening. One neither understands nor helps the oppressed simply by weeping over graphic accounts of their torture. We should weep, but we should not let our tears prevent us from seeing that what is being done is essentially the same as what is being done, in a more discreet and less bloody manner, in all capitalist countries. It is not possible to overcome the excesses without changing the whole, because these ex-cesses are 'necessary' in some countries in order to produce the same effect produced by more 'civilized' methods in Western capitalist countries.

South Africa and Guatemala are both primarily capitalist countries: just as the excesses of the South African system are not caused by racism, neither are those in Guatemala caused by the fact that there is a military govern-ment. The military government in Guatemala was installed through a US-backed coup precisely to protect the United States' capitalist interests. Like South African capitalism, and Latin American capitalism in general, Guatemalan capitalism was established by the colonial subjugation of the indigenous people and they have all (with the exception of Cuba), but Guatemala in particular, remained 'dependent societies for whom only the poles of decision of which they are the object have changed at different his-torical moments – Portugal, Spain, England or the United States' (Freire,

Cultural Action for Freedom, p. 61). They were established, as Freire says, as closed societies, which are

> characterized by a rigid hierarchical social structure, by the lack of internal markets, since their economy is controlled from the outside; by the exportation of raw materials and importation of manufactured goods, without a voice in either process; by a precarious and selective educational system whose schools are an instrument of maintaining the status quo; by high percentages of illiteracy and disease, including the naively named 'tropical diseases' which are really diseases of under-development and dependence; by alarming rates of infant mortality; by malnutrition, often with irreparable effects on mental facilities; by a low life-expectancy, and by a high rate of crime (ibid.).

People born into such a closed society tend to accept it and to 'attribute the sources of such facts and situations in their lives either to some super-reality or to something within themselves'. Religion is one of the 'tools' that has been used to perpetuate this consciousness of 'quasi-adherence' to the status quo. It is not surprising that priests figure prominently among the 'leaders of public opinion' who are imprisoned or killed, since they are teaching that Christianity is really about transforming the world, and so are a very real threat to the status quo.

The colonizers were able to co-opt some of the population into the system to see to its efficient running for them, and from these has developed the present relatively affluent middle class, who are rewarded with a larger share of the national income than the mass of the population. The inequality, however gross, could be maintained to the degree that the latter 'accepted' it. Although these societies are 'closed', they are not static and 'once societies enter the period of transition, immediately the first movements of emergence of the hitherto submerged and silent masses begin to manifest themselves ... [which] forces the power elite to experiment with new forms of maintaining the masses in silence' (ibid., p. 64). By the time this happens the elite has appropriated to itself virtually all the national wealth and the main part of the national income, which in capitalist terms they must be free to do. Where, as in Guatemala, the people are prevented from organizing as workers, nothing can be done to change this state of affairs or even to prevent it from getting worse. In Guatemala the main source of wealth is land, and the growing poverty and landlessness are 'often the consequence of social and economic policies which have deliberately maintained the marginal status of the peasantry in order to guarantee a cheap labour force for the large agricultural estates' (Roger Plant,

Guatemala: Unnatural Disaster, p. 64). When the silence of the masses was broken, even by a moderate voice speaking on their behalf – such as that of President Arbenz in his proposed agrarian reforms (1952–4) – the dominant interest group 'experimented' by having the CIA organize a coup against the 'communist' President. The disparity in the ownership of land between the top 10 per cent of Guatemala's population, who own nearly 80 per cent, and the rest of the population is far greater even than it is between Whites and Blacks in South Africa; there is little difference in the disproportionate share of income received by the 'elite' and by the mass of the population.

Given, on the one hand, this gross inequality, which is the 'natural' progression of capitalism, and, on the other, the United States' determination (which has been renewed under Reagan) to prevent any agrarian or other reforms because of the dangers of communism and the consequent threat to capitalist interests, together with the virtual absence of organized labour, what else can the workers and peasants do but resort to political and other means of wresting their share from the capitalists; and how else can the government control them and protect the interests of the capitalists except by political repression? The repression *has* to be severe, though it does not *have* to take the form of shooting people. Stopping the government's death squads from shooting people will not stop the oppression. That will continue as long as capitalism continues and it will continue in an equally brutal way for as long as the present form of Guatemalan capitalism continues. And, as has been said in another but similar Latin American context, 'the model of a different society is not going to emerge by imposing the values of an "enlightened" elite of whatever nature, whether a political party, a handful of heroes, reforming saints, or whatever, but from conscious and collective action, organized at the grass roots' (São Paulo Justice and Peace Commission, *São Paulo Growth and Poverty*, p. 125). In other words, from the very people who are being arrested and killed in Guatemala by a government which at least has a greater appreciation of their worth and importance than that shown either by Amnesty or by Power. Once a programme for the systematic elimination of such people is embarked upon, then even greater excesses will occur, as they do in Guatemala. In order to make sure of eliminating one person the government forces are prepared to kill any number of people.

Political repression – whether in Western democratic countries, in racist South Africa or in militarily ruled Guatemala – is carefully planned; it is planned by those who reject any interference with their own individual freedom which would result from economic planning to bring about equality. The repression does not simply co-exist with capitalism in its various forms; it is a necessary consequence of it in any form. When this is added to the economic inequality which it is designed to perpetuate, we have a situation of systematic oppression, the degree of which is determined by the origin, nature and degree of inequality. Western capitalist countries are oppressive both in themselves and because of their relationship with other more obviously and grossly oppressive capitalist countries.

Gross oppression is not always very obvious, except to the victims themselves. South Africa is known to be a violent, grossly oppressive country, but it is certainly not obvious to the observer; it has become part of the way of life. Even in Guatemala with its daily killings, Jonathan Power found that in downtown Guatemala City 'the atmosphere, superficially at least, was easy-going ... compared with Belfast, for example, the army presence is relatively unobtrusive'. I mention this not out of any desire to minimize the extent of oppression in these countries but simply to point out that if it is possible to walk down the streets of Guatemala City or Johannesburg without being shot or arrested, the fact that one can do the same in London does not prove that there is no oppression in Britain.

The drawing of an exaggerated picture of the oppressive nature of everyday life in countries like South Africa or Guatemala serves to justify the Western way of life and to strengthen the belief that there must be an essential difference between Western capitalism and the regimes governing these countries. If capitalism was to blame for oppression, then Britain would be oppressive and we would all be immediately aware of it. The Whites in South Africa use the same arguments, and doubtless the elite in Guatemala does. They do not see the oppression partly because it is physically removed from them and partly because they do not want to see it. The same is true in Western countries; only the scale and the proportions are different. But in any capitalist country, whether the minority exploit the majority or vice versa, nobody is free and either the minority or, more usually, the majority is oppressed. They are not free and they are not equal, either materially or before the law – especially before the law, which is one form of equality that even the most extreme individualist claims to recognize. That is the price that *has* to be paid for individual freedom as understood in Western individualistic capitalist terms. 'No price is too high for individual freedom' is a good slogan for those who do not have to pay it. Even if a price did have to be paid for equality, it could hardly be higher than that presently being paid by the many for the individual freedom of the few. I do not believe that human beings have *necessarily* to pay any price for equality; the fact that they do so in practice is due to the strength of the forces ranged against those who are struggling for equality, not to any inherent conflict between freedom and equality. *Pace* Solzhenitsyn and many others, it is of capitalism that oppression is an integral part.

SOCIALISM AND OPPRESSION

In socialist theory the only 'freedom' that has to be sacrificed in the cause of equality is the freedom to exploit others; freedom of expression, freedom to dissent and freedom of conscience are not a threat to socialism unless they are exercised to deny the essential equality of all human beings. If they are so exercised they are not, as we have seen, *human* rights. In practice, however, socialist states have denied not only individual rights in the Western sense but also human rights; they have also not achieved, and cannot achieve, equality if they continue to deny *human* rights. They are as indivisible for socialists as they are for anybody else.

That there is political repression on a vast scale in socialist countries cannot be doubted. It would not help my argument or my conscience to attempt to minimize it. If any degree of oppression is essential to socialism, then not only are extreme instances bound to occur but also it cannot be the vehicle for bringing about the transformation of society. It is my contention that any oppression, however much or little, results from a malfunctioning of socialism. I believe only that man is *not yet* perfect. I have no difficulty, therefore, in admitting even gross imperfections in present forms of socialist society. The exaggeration of these imperfections does not help to overcome them; that simply serves to reinforce and to 'justify' capitalist oppression. If the West, as I have said, has a vested interest in exaggerating the degree of oppression even in other capitalist countries, this is even more evident in regard to socialist ones and to the Soviet Union in particular. Consider, for example, the capital made out of the refusal of the Soviet government to allow Lisa Alexeyeva to go to America to be with her husband, Andrei Sakharov's stepson, and of the drama of Sakharov's hunger-strike. I would agree both that the refusal was wrong and that Sakharov's action was a very noble one. (I would not invert the double standards of those who considered Sakharov a hero and the IRA hunger-strikers suicidal political blackmailers.) But in South Africa, for example, literally hundreds of thousands of women are prevented by law from being with their husbands. They cannot even go to another part of their own country to be with them, let alone to a foreign one. There is no point in their going on hunger-strike; they are starving already. Not one of them, however, makes the front page of British newspapers.

Far more attention is given to the Soviet Union by governments, the media and by Amnesty International than to any other country. The Soviet Union has about 6 per cent of the world's population, but some 14 per cent of Amnesty's adopted prisoners. Peter Benenson pointed out when he founded Amnesty in 1961 that if the United States had opposed the tyranny of Spain and Portugal with as much energy as it opposed Cuba, Agostino Neto and thousands like him would not have been in prison; and that if the Soviet Union had not been threatened by the nuclear build-up in the West, they would have granted at least some of the claims of the dissidents.

We will look at the present facts, but this cannot be done in isolation nor simply in the light of Western individualistic norms. Even the scale of repression must be seen in perspective. Amnesty's 1981 Report states, for example, that it learned of approximately two hundred people being arrested in the Soviet Union during the year for the non-violent exercise of their human rights. A proportionate figure would be five in Guatemala, where more than twice that number are being killed every day. Nothing, except perhaps Hitler's 'resettlement' programme, can compare with the Stalinist pogroms and purges. The present scale of repression in the Soviet Union itself bears no comparison with that. Stalinism was not, however, an extreme form of socialism; it was a fanatical concentration on one aspect of socialism which was exacerbated by more 'material' factors. For Stalin no price was too high to pay for economic development, just as, for capitalists, no price is too high for their own individual liberty. But whereas the capitalist insistence on their understanding of individual liberty is essential to capitalism, the Stalinist economistic understanding of man is not. That too denies man a role in transforming society and subjects him to a mechanistic process. For the capitalist, the development of the whole man can never be realized; for the Stalinist, that is for the future, once the economic development has been completed; for the socialist, man transforms himself *in* transforming society.

None of this in any way excuses the abuses which are perpetuated in the Soviet Union; nor are they excused by the fact that the Revolution took place in the most industrially backward state in Europe and consequently every effort had to be devoted to catching up with the capitalists in capitalist terms. But the existence of such abuses does not prove the superiority of the Western capitalist system. Many of the dissidents are undoubtedly a threat to the present limited, distorted view of socialism; others are opposed to any form of socialism; some, however, appear simply to be victims of the Party's belief in its own propaganda. When genuine criticism is feared, criticism is feared everywhere. Some of the documents which people are imprisoned for writing or possessing are no more threatening even to the present Soviet system than *Black Beauty* was to the South African government, which banned it. One thing that Amnesty's reporting does make clear is that even though the number of dissidents is comparatively small they are not an homogeneous group: they comprise intellectuals and workers, members of nationalist and religious groups, conscientious objectors, trade union and human rights activists. Amnesty's 1981 Report notes that the major drive against all categories of dissidents launched at the end of 1979 continued into the first four months of 1981:

> Forms of repression within Amnesty International's mandate have hit three types of dissenter especially hard: 'Helsinki Monitors', unofficial groups trying to monitor Soviet compliance with human rights provisions of the Final Act of the 1975 Helsinki Conference on Security and Co-operation in Europe; critics of the Soviet nationalities policy in the non-Russian Soviet Republics and advocates of political independence for their nations, particularly Ukrainians, Lithuanians and Estonians; and religious believers, particularly Baptists, Seventh-Day Adventists, Pentecostalists and Russian Orthodox believers (p. 378).

Another point which Amnesty highlights is the severity of the sentences and the harshness of the treatment meted out to dissidents. The treatment is harsh by any standards; it appears even harsher when viewed through Western middle-class eyes. The conditions in the labour camps would probably not strike an African migrant worker living in an overcrowded hostel and working in a mine as any more horrific than his own; and he hasn't even been accused of any crime. People whom we call criminals in the West might also have a different view. This is not to excuse the conditions; but, in regard to any country which has a different tradition and culture, we cannot assume that everybody views such things as forms of punishment in the same way as we do. Nevertheless, even if it were necessary to restrict the freedom of some individuals because they were genuinely acting against the interests of other people, it would not be necessary for it to be done in the way the Soviet system does it. Bad conditions are exacerbated by the climate, for which even the present system cannot be blamed, and by the long distances over which prisoners are transported. It is quite normal, reports Amnesty, for prisoners to be in transit for a month

or more, with sometimes as many as thirty people packed into a compart-
ment meant for only eight or ten, and with only the most meagre rations;
according to the regulations they are to receive a warm meal only every
fourth day. Although torture is not systematically practised in the Soviet
Union as it is, particularly, in many Latin American countries, Amnesty's
Report on Torture noted that 'as hunger is [thus] used as a deliberate
instrument to destroy the physical and psychological morale of the prisoner,
the diet may be considered to be a form of torture' (p. 188). In 1980
conditions 'continued to be characterized by chronic hunger, overwork in
difficult conditions, inadequate medical treatment and arbitrary deprivation of the limited rights to correspondence and family visits' (ibid., p. 333).
Prisoners of conscience in a corrective labour colony 'protested in Septem-
ber 1980 that conditions were calculated to bring about their "gradual
psychological and physical destruction"' (ibid.). In the psychiatric hospitals
in which some dissidents are detained, torture, as Amnesty's Report says,
is an administrative practice. Drugs are administered not only to 'encourage' recantations of political views but also as punishment.

Incidents like the following, reported by Leonid Plyushch after his
release from Dnepropetrovsk Psychiatric Hospital in 1976, appear in
numerous accounts by former prisoners of conscience:

'One of the patients called the doctors Gestapoists [sic]. They pre-
scribed injections of sulphur. (After an injection of sulphur your tempera-
ture goes up to 40 degrees, the place where you had the injection is very
painful, you cannot get away from the pain. Many people get haemor-
rhoids as a result of sulphur injections.) This patient groaned loudly for
24 hours, mad with pain he tried to hide himself under the bed, in despair
he broke the window and tried to cut his throat with the glass. Then he
was punished again and beaten up. He kept asking everyone, "Am I going
to die?" And only when he did begin to die and another patient noticed
it did they stop the sulphur. And for two days they gave him oxygen and
brought him various medicines' (AI Report on Prisoners of Conscience
in the USSR, pp. 199–200).

The insanity of the system, rather than of the inmates, is attested by the
actions which lead to committal – 'giving song recitals in one's own flat ...
persistently making religious craft articles, writing complaints to government authorities; and the diagnoses of the officially appointed psychiatrists:
"nervous exhaustion brought on by her search for justice ... delusional
ideas of reformism and struggle within the existing social political system
in the USSR ... mania for reconstructing society"' (p. 184).

A large proportion of dissidents – about half of those arrested during the period covered by Amnesty's 1981 Report – are religious believers. 'All religious groups in the USSR live under important restrictions imposed by the state, which is committed to the withering away of religion' (ibid., p. 30). I have argued elsewhere that atheism and the rejection of Christianity is not essential to a Marxist understanding of socialism and is in fact inconsistent with Marx's own historical materialism. The practical compatibility between Christianity and Marxism has been amply demonstrated in Latin America, in Nicaragua in particular. The Soviets, however, have adopted Lenin's more militantly anti-religious stance; though Lenin himself did not advocate an anti-religion crusade. Although he maintained that, as far as the *state* was concerned, religion was a purely private matter, he also maintained that, as far as the *Party* was concerned, the struggle against religion was not a private matter. He did not, as the Amnesty Report states, deny the former when he advocated the latter. In the Soviet system the Party is identified with the state, so that while the Constitution recognizes the right to freedom of conscience and to conduct religious worship, the struggle against religion is part of official policy. The decree 'On Religious Associations' demands that

> all religious congregations be registered with the Council for Religious Affairs – permission be obtained for the use of a prayer building. Congregations are forbidden to organize special gatherings of children, young people or women [surely unsocialist sexism] for prayer or other purposes, to organize Bible meetings, literature meetings, handicraft meetings, work meetings or meetings for religious study, to organize groups, circles or departments, to organize excursions or children's facilities, to open libraries or reading rooms or to organize sanatoria or medical assistance.

Children may be, and have been, removed from their parents and taken into the care of the state if the parents are considered to have failed in their duty 'to educate them in the spirit of the moral code of the builder of communism'.

The fact that the Soviet government 'needs' deliberately to suppress religion proves either that it is not a socialist state or that religion is not what Marx and Lenin said it was. If religion were simply an opiate of (or for) the people, they would not need it once they had woken up to economic reality in a socialist society; it would simply disappear once the infrastructure which gave rise to it was changed. If, however, it persists even in a socialist state, where there is no economic alienation, it cannot be simply the sublimation of such alienation; there would be nothing for it to legitimize. The Soviet and South African governments agree in giving their own remarkably similar definitions of religion as being concerned only with 'otherworldly things'. Any actions which go beyond that are seen by both as a rejection of religion for politics. These actions are entering the field of politics, but they do not entail the rejection of religion, which the Soviets would welcome and the South Africans regret. If religion is concerned only with otherworldly things, it is no threat to any political system, as the South Africans well understand; if it is not – which is proved when it persists in a socialist system – then Marxists need to examine the claim and practice of those who find in religion, and particularly in Christianity, a motive for revolutionary concern with this world; the practice must be judged, both by Christians and Marxists, in political terms.

The fundamentalist sects which reject the authority of the state, for example, may be being more authentically Marxist than the Soviet Communist Party. Many of the actions of religious dissidents might well be 'political' rather than 'religious', according to the Party's definitions, but they do not become criminal just because they are performed by people who claim to be religious. Religious belief, on the other hand, does not provide an excuse for violating the rights of others and its practice may be subjected to the same restrictions as apply to other beliefs; and a religion which is based on love for all men can hardly object to that. But the Party is not 'all men'. Some believers, however, are persecuted simply for practising religion in the Party's sense. Any religious teaching or propaganda is seen as a threat to atheistic propaganda, which has assumed the legitimizing role of religion. This does not mean that the churches have been completely suppressed; on the contrary, according to many observers they flourish and display a greater vitality than the churches in many Western countries.

In socialist countries the main issue is political repression rather than economic coercion. In any form of society limits are placed on freedom of the individual person by the needs of others. Capitalist societies, as we have seen, are not free, because limits are imposed through political structures which protect the 'right' of the few to perpetuate inequality, and thus also to restrict the freedom of both the exploited and the exploiters either directly or under the guise of impersonal market forces. This does not just happen; it *must* happen once the right of people to be unequal is accepted. For the socialist a free society is one in which '(a) the limits are as wide as possible; (b) each individual has a say in deciding where it is necessary for those limits to be; and (c) each individual knows how and why she/he is being limited' (Turner, *The Eye of the Needle*, p. 48). Such a society is not only compatible with, but is essential to, equality in society. But, just as repression and inequality do not just happen but require planning, so do freedom and equality. The purpose of this planning is to prevent just the abuse of freedom which we have seen is the necessary consequence of capitalism. This, however, is not what has happened in socialist countries in general, and in the Soviet Union in particular. Planning requires planners, but the planners have become superior to, and separate from, the people. The Soviet Union, says Richard Turner, is probably the classical example of the failure to deal with the two main problems of planning.

> The first is to prevent those individuals who, being at the top of the necessary decision hierarchy, have more power, from using the power to their own material advantage. This is something which may be done consciously, through corruption, but also can occur gradually and unconsciously. Feeling important, and having high prestige, it is very easy to accept unconsciously that one should go immediately to the head of the queue, that one needs a chauffeur-driven car 'to save time parking', that one needs a specially comfortable apartment because one is subject to special tensions, and because one often has to work at home. Insensibly, convincing rationalizations of this sort can produce an elite who have a vested interest in maintaining their positions.
>
> The second problem, which shades into the first, is to ensure that the decision-makers do not, through the very nature of their jobs, become isolated from the people, unaware of what the people want, and, hiding behind a hedge of technical jargon, perhaps no longer even able to communicate with ordinary people (ibid., p. 54).

The Soviet bureaucrats have not simply failed to keep in touch with the people, they quite deliberately do not do so, because the people would not be likely to agree to the demands being made on them as workers; not in their own interests, but in order to enable the Soviet Union to compete with the West.

It is not the *need* for planning which is the cause of repression but the way in which it has been and is being done. The Soviet Union is 'guilty' when judged according to socialist norms of freedom and equality, which is more important than the fact that it does not conform to the Western understanding of individual rights.

The reason for Amnesty International's particular concern about the Soviet Union is, I think, that it believes that the provisions for the violation of human rights are enshrined in the Constitution and in the criminal code. A cursory glance at its detailed Report on Prisoners of Conscience in the USSR would give the impression that because of the nature of the law every other citizen has been subject to arrest and imprisonment. In fact it deals with about four hundred people who were arrested over a period of four years, virtually all of whom are mentioned by name; a similarly detailed report on Guatemala would require a series of volumes about the size of the *Encyclopaedia Britannica*. Amnesty's method is very similar to that of Solzhenitsyn, which has been described as 'an unreconciled concatenation of bare facts and supposition' (Frances Barker, in *New Blackfriars*, April 1975). Despite the detailed information which Amnesty has from official sources, from the scores of former prisoners of conscience who have left the USSR, and from the profusion of *samizdat* publications, it 'believes the real number of prisoners of conscience in the USSR to be much larger than the known number' (A I Report on Prisoners of Conscience in the USSR, p. 1). It has no more grounds for this belief than Solzhenitsyn had for saying: 'Knowing the sense and spirit of the Revolution, it is easy to *guess* that during these months [October and November 1917] such central prisons as Kresty and Petrograd and the Butyrki in Moscow, and many provincial prisons like Rem were filled' (*The Gulag Archipelago*, p. 26). Perhaps they share a mystic perception of reality. Amnesty also uses Solzhenitsyn's ploy of using the same evidence to illustrate different aspects of repression, thus giving the impression of a greater number of cases. Leonid Plyushch, for example, is introduced three times as 'a Ukrainian cyberneticist who was imprisoned from 1973 to 1976'. The report is a typical example of dealing with isolated facts and throws very little light on the problem of oppression which is undoubtedly there. It could in fact give the opposite impression and allow people to dismiss the 400 as cranks. It states, for example, that 'virtually any unauthorized criticism of official action or policy or distribution of information on "forbidden" subjects may lead to imprisonment'. If that is the case, yet only 400 out of 265 million people were arrested in the course of four years, it could be argued that there is a very low level of criticism and that therefore there cannot be very much wrong with the system as a whole. But there is. What is wrong is not the framing of the Constitution and the law. Amnesty, however, has taken Solzhenitsyn's advice: 'For several centuries we had a proverb: "Don't fear the law, fear the judge".' But, in my opinion, it is time to reverse the proverb: 'Don't fear the judge, fear the law.'

The Soviet government claims, as the Amnesty Report notes, that its new Constitution, which was promulgated in 1977, ' "fully guarantees and ensures the practical implementation in the Soviet Union of all the principles [sic] enshrined in the Charter of the United Nations, the International Covenant on Civil and Political Rights, the International Covenant on

Economic, Social and Cultural Rights and other international instruments of the United Nations concerning human rights" '. In Amnesty International's view the new Constitution, like that of 1936, institutionalizes unjustifiable restrictions on Soviet citizens' human rights. Such a view can only be held on the assumption that *any* (not just the Soviet) form of socialism is wrong. The Report states:

> According to Article 50, Soviet citizens are guaranteed freedom of expression in various forms. However, as in the 1936 Constitution, this guarantee is prefaced by the statement that these rights are guaranteed 'in accordance with the interest of the people and in order to strengthen and develop the socialist system'. The judicial and other authorities have made plain that the prefacing statement restricts the manner in which these rights may be used.

Of course it does, but, as I said in Chapter 3, all the international instruments of the United Nations have such a restriction. *All* the rights recognized in the Universal Declaration of Human Rights are limited by the rights of others and by the just requirements not only of morality and public order but also of the 'general welfare in a democratic society'. Amnesty's own position may be so absolutist that it believes that no government is ever justified in restricting the individual rights of anyone in any way, but it cannot claim that any government which does so is thereby violating internationally agreed principles. Far less can it claim, particularly as an apolitical organization, that this only applies to socialist governments. (Amnesty's 1981 Annual Report commenting on South Korea's new Constitution pointed out that it guaranteed certain freedoms. 'However, these rights may be restricted constitutionally "when necessary for national security, the maintenance of law and order for public welfare" in violation of the International Covenant on Civil and Political Rights.' An errata slip instructed readers to delete 'in violation of ...'. No such instruction was given when similar statements were made about socialist countries.) The Report goes on to quote Soviet commentators who 'have come close to acknowledging the Soviet government's restrictive attitude to Soviet citizens' human rights':

> Soviet laws afford our citizens broad political freedoms. At the same time they protect our system and the interest of the Soviet people from any attempts to abuse these freedoms. It is a norm of our life that the exercise of rights and freedoms is inseparable from citizens' fulfilment of their obligations to society.

... a man must live and act in correspondence with the highest humanistic goals and ideals of society – to fulfil the norms and rules of socialist life at work and at home, to struggle with violations of these norms, in all ways to support everything that corresponds to the nature of socialism and to help speed up the movement of society towards communism.

If 'British' were substituted for 'Soviet' and 'Western democracy' for 'socialism', I am sure that Amnesty would have no objection to the above as statements of principle. Amnesty, however, examines the principles in the light of what happens and so condemns the principles. But the principles are not to blame for what happens. Nor are the laws which follow from them. Soviet law forbids, among other things, any 'agitation or propaganda carried on for the purpose of subverting or weakening the Soviet regime or of committing particular, especially dangerous crimes against the state or the circulation for the same purpose of slanderous fabrications which defame the Soviet state and social system or the circulation, or preparation or keeping, for the same purpose, of literature of such content'.

About a quarter of the people with whom Amnesty's Report is concerned were imprisoned for 'anti-Soviet agitation or propaganda' or 'dissemination of fabrications'. These people were not imprisoned *because* of such laws as that quoted, and they would not be helped even if Amnesty were successful in its appeals to have such laws repealed. They were arrested because of the interpretation given to those laws within the present system. It is the system which is wrong, not the Constitution or the laws. In imprisoning such people the Soviet Union is not acting in accordance with its own principles and its own laws. This is not because it violates them in particular instances, but because the whole present system is based on the substitution of the interests of the Party for the interests of the people, the Soviet Union and socialism. The state, instead of 'withering away', has become more and more firmly entrenched. Far from moving towards 'the dictatorship of the proletariat' or even to any form of democracy, it has become more and more centralized within the bureaucratic machinery of the Party. When people are arrested for 'anti-Soviet agitation', therefore, what in fact they are being arrested for is anti-Party agitation. But a bureaucracy, whether it is a Western democratic government, a military dictatorship or a Communist Party, does not have rights; only other people have rights. If the Soviet state were genuinely protecting the interests of the Soviet people (which is the principle enunciated in the Constitution), and if the 100 people who were arrested were acting against the interests of the other 265 million people, then their restriction would be justified, both in socialist terms and in accordance with the UN International Covenants, since an individual is not free to act against the interest of other people.

The difference between the traditional Western understanding and a socialist one is that the former is based on a preconceived idea of what those interests are, whereas in the latter they can only be worked out in practice. But it cannot be worked out if a particular group sets itself up as the sole criterion of truth and correct practice. Socialism cannot be dogmatic; totalitarianism, whether of the right or the left, always is. Dogmatism is opposed to any change; it cannot, therefore, be a necessary stage of the progress towards a fully socialist society. Amnesty and the Soviet government are equally dogmatic, so there is little to be gained from their shouting at one another. While Amnesty is ideologically opposed to any form of socialist morality, the Soviet Union has reduced it to a rule of thumb: the Party is always right.

At the very least, it cannot be *proved* that the dissidents have acted against the interests of the people, because nobody knows what those interests are – the people have never been consulted and there is no provision for their being consulted. No matter what 'slander' or 'agitation' a person indulges in, therefore, there must be at least some doubt about his or her guilt. So all those who have been arrested are entitled to be presumed innocent. Within the present system it is not surprising that, as Amnesty repeatedly points out, a Soviet Court has never acquitted anybody charged with a political or religious offence. (There do, however, appear to be exceptions. Anatol Levitin Krasnov, an Orthodox priest, who was arrested in 1969, was freed by the Supreme Court after the local court had found that, despite several months of pre-trial investigation, there was insufficient evidence to support the prosecution's allegation: 'He holds a hostile, anti-Soviet position and should be imprisoned like some sectarians.' *See* J. A. Brown in *New Blackfriars*, June, 1974.) Those concerned are doubtless guilty of acting against the interests of the Party as defined by the Party. Amnesty would, I believe, have more success even within its limited sphere if it were to acknowledge that in imprisoning offenders the Court and the Party are acting contrary to the interests of socialism. This would be no more political than the false assumption it makes that abuse of human rights in capitalist countries has nothing to do with the capitalist system itself.

Many of the dissidents themselves would not agree that their imprisonment is the necessary and inevitable consequence of socialism, since their 'crime' is the criticism of the government on socialist grounds. Even

Solzhenitsyn was a Marxist when he was first arrested. Anatol Levitin, who spent seven years (1949–56) in a labour camp, and who was relieved of his post as teacher in 1966 for criticizing the government and went to prison again for three years in 1971, remained a dedicated socialist: 'From childhood I revolted against all kinds of barriers fabricated by people ... I was a supporter of revolution but always repelled by its atrocities ... There can be no socialism without democracy.' When he was released from prison, he and others issued a document from the 'Initiative Group for the Defence of Human Rights in the Soviet Union' in which they said that they had never tried to discredit the social aims of the government of the country; they were 'only opposed to those actions of the authorities which would be considered inadmissible under any social system and any government'. Two of the authors had been forced to make false statements at their trial admitting anti-Soviet activities. 'It is tragic,' the document says, 'that these lies are affecting the fate and reputation of all the political prisoners in camps, prisons and mental hospitals in the Soviet Union' (Brown, ibid.). Because the whole system is founded on the lie that the Party and the interests of the Party are synonymous with the state and the interests of the people then any real opposition to it must, in the eyes of the Party, be 'lies'. But it is the lie, not the Constitution nor the fact that it purports to be a socialist system, which is responsible for the suppression of dissent. The defence of *human* rights is a threat to the Soviet system, but the system cannot be changed by incorporating a Western individualistic understanding of rights into the Constitution.

This would only lead to the replacement of one elite with another. Provided the replacement was a capitalist one, Amnesty and other critics, including some of the dissidents, would be satisfied. Socialism is not concerned with which elite should rule; it actually believes that people can rule themselves without the 'help' of any elite. Some of the anti-socialist dissidents doubtless feel that what is wrong with the Soviet system is not that it is run by an elite, but that it is the wrong sort of elite. Not all of them share Levitin's 'feeling of kinship ... towards simple Russian people' and his antipathy towards intellectuals. It is not possible to say how many of them share the classist view expressed by Solzhenitsyn:

> How could the *engineers* accept the *dictatorship* of the workers, their subordinates in industry, so little skilled or trained, and comprehending neither the physical nor the economic laws of production, but now occupying the top positions from which they supervised the *engineers*? Why shouldn't the engineers have considered it more natural for the

structure of society to be headed by those who could intelligently direct its activity? (*The Gulag Archipelago*, p. 390.)

It is not 'natural' for the structure of society to be headed by anybody and it is not socialist for it to be headed by an elite, whether they be engineers, intellectuals, workers or Party members. Capitalists and upholders of the present Soviet system alike believe that the few have the right to decide what is for the good of the many; they differ only in who the 'few' should be.

A perfect socialist society cannot be created overnight, but it cannot be created at all by anti-socialist means. Repression in the Soviet Union is not part of the transition process to a socialist system; Soviet socialism does not suffer from growing pains, it suffers from cramp. A socialist system, even one aimed at creating perfect equality, not only should not but cannot be imposed. If people have a right to share equally in the society once it is created, they also have an equal right to determine how it should be created; if this right is not respected it is impossible to create a system which protects the interests of all the people. Neither governments nor individuals are free to deny people this right in the name of a party, or of an elite or of their own individual liberty. If socialism is to serve the interests of all the people, it must provide for different and even competing interests; it must, therefore make positive provision for dissent and debate.

'A society is to that extent socialist in which it provides the possibilities for a free or creative development of every individual' (Gajo Petrovic, in Kolakowski and Hampshire (eds.), *The Socialist Idea*, p. 100). And only the people themselves can define those possibilities. Democracy is not only compatible with socialism, it is essential to a genuinely socialist and free society, as defined above. It is absent from the Soviet system, which perpetuates the Stalinist pursuit of economic progress at the expense of liberty. This, however, is the inversion of capitalist ideology, which upholds liberty at the expense of equality, not its contradiction. Even if the Soviets were prepared to recognize the failings of their present system, they would doubtless prefer it to a Western capitalist form of democracy. Amnesty's implied advocacy of the latter as an alternative may well serve only to harden the Soviet government's resolve to continue along its present path. In demanding too much – the complete rejection of socialism – Amnesty destroys the chance of achieving its own limited aim: the prevention of human suffering. This suffering is caused by the totalitarian, not the socialist, nature of the present system.

The system is basically the same in the other East European states, though the 'line' is sometimes softened and individual dissent is either not so prevalent or not so severely repressed. The former appears to be the case in Hungary – not simply because of the fear of a repetition of the events of 1956; increased prosperity also doubtless plays its part. In Czechoslovakia those who are arrested tend to be prominent, outspoken critics of the regime; other would-be dissenters are controlled by more subtle means, rather like they are in the West. Socialism in Yugoslavia has not yet found an alternative to suppressing the nationalist claims and feelings of the various full-scale national groups of which it is now comprised. This suppression has been extended to an orthodox priest who 'took advantage of the religious ceremony of the christening of his son to sing at his house ... nationalist songs and to incite those present to chauvinist euphoria'. (I am writing this a few days after the declaration of martial law in Poland which provides further proof, if any were needed, of the depth of the conflict between the 'needs' of bureaucratic socialism and the interests of the workers. *Any* control by the workers is a threat to totalitarian control by the Party and is bound ultimately to lead to some form of confrontation. I do not think any purpose would be served by commenting on the current confrontation and I am not ill-advised enough to forecast developments.) Little is known of what happens in Bulgaria and Albania.

It is unlikely, perhaps impossible, that the other countries in Eastern Europe will be fully liberated and fully socialist until the Soviet Union is. Since the conditions that gave rise to uprisings in Hungary, Czechoslovakia and Poland are also present in the Soviet Union, and the conflict between the people and the Party even sharper and more oppressive, this is not necessarily a counsel of despair. For the same reason, repression in these countries is not simply a carbon-copy of that in the Soviet Union, though the difference is primarily one of degree, since the Soviet influence and threat hangs over all these. The Soviet's belief in socialism in one nation results in the imposition of its form of socialism on its satellites. Its hegemony over them is the international equivalent of the Party's hegemony over the people of the Soviet Union.

The West has never shown any great understanding of or sympathy for China. A sixteenth-century missionary, Matteo Ricci, recognized that they had their own very different and highly developed culture and that it was not possible to implant a form of Christianity based on Greek and scholastic philosophy and on Western understanding of ritual. It took the Vatican a couple of hundred years to realize that he was right. Many people, including Amnesty, have still not come to a similar conclusion as far as politics and human rights are concerned. Even the most sympathetic picture of life in China under communist rule is probably not very appealing to Western eyes; but it does not have to be. The important question, and one that is impossible to answer, is: What does it look like to Chinese eyes? Those whose voices are heard are likely to be those who disapprove of the present system. Edgar Snow, writing of life in China in 1970, describes the man in the street, whom he calls Citizen Wang, as

> being well fed, healthy, adequately clothed, fully employed with labour tasks, Mao classes, and technical studies, during his six-day work week ... In the city he accepts discipline from his Party-line neighbourhood committee, responsible for child care, sanitation and pollution control, settling disputes, welfare, health, and provision for aged and handicapped people ... Citizen Wang lives on a very narrow budget but is free from bank mortgages, debt and the fear of starvation and beggary which plagued his parents (*China's Long Revolution*, p. 31).

The army, he says, is omnipresent, but the behaviour of the armed forces is exemplary and they are 'ever ready to help in emergencies in field or factory'. He says little about political repression; though he does note that Chairman Mao himself was most unhappy about the maltreatment of 'captives' during the Cultural Revolution.

The full extent of such maltreatment is still not known, but Amnesty's 1980 Report quotes Vice-Premier Deng Xiaoping as saying: 'According to incomplete statistics, 2,900,000 people have now been rehabilitated and many more have been rehabilitated whose cases were not put on file or tried.' Mao, according to Snow, estimated that 95 per cent of the population supported him and his policies; but 5 per cent of the 700 million people of whom he was speaking is still a lot of people. The 'rehabilitation' even of three million people, however, is not the same as 'the near abolition of personal freedoms and the creation of a repressive machine that was often arbitrary and on occasion quite savage' (Power, *Against Oblivion*, p. 136). In the fifty years before the establishment of the People's Republic of China, over 40 million Chinese people were killed – in the Sino-Japanese war, in civil wars and famines; when the communists took over four million people were dying every year of infections and parasitic diseases. A few years before the take-over, under the Nationalist regime, 'a wild inflation had destroyed the value of the currency; corruption was flagrant and open, morale was falling. The oppressive police repression in the name of anti-communism was taking victims, usually men of liberal views and creating an atmosphere of fear and despair in all classes.' The atmosphere had been building up throughout the twenty years of Chiang Kai-shek's extermination campaigns against Chinese communists For hundreds of years before that there had been a history of peasant rebellions over the distribution of land and the extortionate practices of the landlords. 'The social system was therefore unstable in the economic sense, but rigid in the class structure. Land ownership went with scholarship, literacy, the monopoly of government posts and higher education. Tenancy and small ownership connoted illiteracy, poverty, often hunger, oppression, superstition and latent rebellion' (Fitzgerald, *Communism Takes China*, pp. 9–10). This does not justify the undoubted excesses of the communists, but they cannot be accused of abolishing something that was not there in the first place, or of creating something that already existed.

Nor can the repression be blamed on a 'hopelessly politicized philosophy' (Power, p. 139). Everybody's philosophy, if it has any practical relevance, is politicized; Mao would doubtless have claimed that his was hopefully politicized. The fact that Mao considered that the concept of 'the people' was not an absolute one does not, as Amnesty claims, put 'into broader perspective the policy of repression of political dissent'; nor does it explain why in particular cases Amnesty can see no reason for people being arrested. I would have thought it self-evident that 'the people' and 'the interests of the people' change according to historical circumstances. People do not exist, and their interests cannot be defined, in the abstract. An action which may further those interests in some circumstances does not necessarily do so in all. But this does not mean that they can be arbitrarily defined in any particular historical circumstances. When they are, as happens in China as well as in the Soviet Union, that is an abuse of the concepts. There would be even more repression if they were absolutized. It is not possible to define once and for all who the 'enemies of the people' are and then to draw up laws which provide for the restriction of only such people. The Sixteen Point Programme of the Cultural Revolution states that the main target 'is those within the Party who are in authority and are taking the capitalist road'. The problem in individual cases is whether the person concerned is taking that path and is thus an 'enemy of the people'; not, as Amnesty suggests, that there cannot be 'enemies of the people'. In practice, many of those arrested are probably not; they simply disagree with the interpretation of those in authority, which, according to the Programme, they should be free to do. 'It is normal for the masses to hold different views. Contention between different views is unavoidable, necessary and beneficial.' Their arrest, therefore, is contrary to, rather than a consequence of, the 'politicized philosophy'. It is a consequence of bureaucracy: 'The organizational principle of the Party is democratic centralism ... the entire Party is subordinate to the Central Committee.'

Mao was fond of resolving contradictions, but he did not resolve the contradiction in the Programme. On the one hand it stated: 'In the Great Proletarian Cultural Revolution, the only method is for the masses to liberate themselves and any method of doing things on their behalf must not be used.' But on the other: 'The outcome of this great cultural revolution will be determined by whether the Party leadership does or does not dare boldly to arouse the masses.' Once again, as in the Soviet Union, it is the Party, not the people, which knows best.

Unlike Stalin, Mao was not ideologically committed to economic progress and industrialization at all costs. He wanted to unite a cultural revolution with increased production. To do this it was 'necessary, first of all, to create public opinion, to do work in the ideological sphere'. To Western ears this doubtless sounds like indoctrination, but then we have been indoctrinated in another ideology. There is no essential difference between being bombarded with advertisements to encourage consumerism and capitalism, and being subjected to the constant repetition of the thoughts of Chairman Mao. Nor is there much difference between the adulation afforded to footballers and pop stars and that given to Mao, which, as Snow notes, was comparatively restrained for people who have been accustomed to Emperor-worship for 2,000 years. Snow suggests that his Citizen Wang's subjection to constant indoctrination with the view that China is politically correct about everything is compensated for by the fact that he is 'not troubled by murder stories, market plunges, pornography, race riots, divorce scandals, dope rings, muggings, commercialized sex, sadism and masochism' (*China's Long Revolution*, p. 32). Even some people in the West might be prepared to sacrifice some of their individual liberty for such a comparatively carefree existence. But there is no need to sacrifice human liberty, which is sacrificed when, contrary to Mao's own teaching, people are not allowed to think for themselves or to have a say in determining their common destiny.

Repression did not end with the passing of Mao in 1976; in fact, Amnesty's 1981 Report states that there has been a 'noticeable deterioration in the human rights situation marked by a number of arbitrary arrests and increased restrictions on civil liberties'. It has been admitted by the government that 'mistakes' had been made and doubtless they still are being made. Information about the overall effects of the system and about the recent attempts at 'liberalization' is still difficult to obtain. Given the history of China it is understandable that Mao was not at all disposed, and his successors only briefly disposed, to be open to the West; given the history of the West it is doubtful whether such openness would be particularly beneficial to the Chinese people.

Vietnam is another socialist country which is something of a mystery to many people in the West. I have already mentioned the thousands who have been detained in 're-education camps' since 1975. The idea of re-education camps is not only foreign, it is repulsive to most Western people. It is strange, however, that the people who are most disgusted by them are the same people who proclaim the virtues of National Service as a means of instilling a sense of discipline in the nation's youth. The training that some have proposed should be given to unemployed people in Britain is much the same as 're-education'. In Vietnam the camp inmates 'have to attend various classes – political, cultural, scientific and technical, professional – and have to learn a profession which will help them earn their living after release'.

I am not recommending re-education camps nor suggesting that they are necessary in any transition to a socialist society. The Vietnamese practice of consigning people to such camps cannot simply be equated, as it is by Amnesty, with imprisoning people without trial in violation of internationally recognized norms. As the Vietnamese government pointed out in its reply to Amnesty's report on its mission to Vietnam: 'There may be different conceptions of humanitarianism and human rights. Ours is this: respect for human rights, in the case of members of the puppet army, should include re-education so as to bring them back to society, and we believe this is possible without resorting to trials. We trust our conception is the right one. However, we would not object to other conceptions of humanitarianism and human rights.' The government maintains that all the 40,000, who represent 3 per cent of the 1.3 million who served the previous regime, were guilty of national treason which could have been punished by a minimum of twenty years' imprisonment or by death. They further point out that 'in Vietnamese psychology the absence of judiciary condemnation spares the person concerned a tarnished judiciary record'. Amnesty's approach, on the other hand, is completely legalistic and it recommended that the whole practice should be abolished. With some justification the government pointed out that since Amnesty had a different conception of human rights and did not really understand the situation, its recommendations were irrelevant. It should have been satisfied with acquainting 'the Vietnamese side with experience from the world, and the Vietnamese side will eventually take a decision on the matter'. Amnesty nevertheless insists that many of those detained in the camps are prisoners of conscience. The Vietnamese government admits that both its legal system and the implementation of the law are far from perfect, so it is most likely that people are detained who should not be, even according to the Vietnamese understanding of human rights. But campaigning on their behalf is an entirely different matter from condemning the practice as such because it does not conform to Western norms. There might well be reasons for condemning it, but neither I nor Amnesty know enough about the whole context to condemn it as categorically as Amnesty does.

The repression that is practised in socialist countries is not the inevitable price that has had to be paid for economic progress. Individuals do not have the right to work against the good of all, and preventing them from doing so is not repression. But in none of the countries mentioned is it possible to know whether those accused were acting against the interest of the people or only of the Party. Even if they were, that would not justify the excessive measures taken. But at least the progress that has been made has not been made *because* of the denial of human rights, as is the case in a capitalist system. Nobody can deny that there has been remarkable progress: we can no longer urge our children to think of the starving millions in China: despite, or perhaps because of, United States 'help', the other Latin American countries do not compare with Cuba for stability and prosperity; the Soviet Union itself has become a highly industrialized society in sixty years.

This does not in itself prove that socialism is better than capitalism; the progress does not compensate for the repression. It does, however, give the lie to the capitalist myth that progress is the result of the initiative of the few whose individual liberty must be preserved at the expense of institutionalized inequality, which would be retained even in a perfect capitalist society. All it proves is that there is not yet a perfect socialist society. So far socialism has been seen primarily, almost exclusively, as an alternative economic system; which is not surprising in countries which have endured hundreds of years of capitalist exploitation. People are then made subservient to economic needs just as they are in capitalist systems; the main difference being that it is done personally rather than by 'impersonal forces'. Bureaucratic socialism has shown that, for the majority of people in a country, socialism is a better economic system. Power, however, has remained in the hands of elites, who use it not only to their own material advantage but also to deprive the people of their *human* right to be both free and equal by determining for themselves how socialism should be practised for and by them.

CHAPTER 8

OPPRESSION AND ELITES

One fact is certain, namely that oppression exists in both capitalist and socialist countries. It is practised on a vast scale in many countries that I have not even mentioned. While it is not possible to quantify it or to say whether there is more in capitalist countries than in socialist ones or vice versa, there are certainly no grounds for the Western myth that oppression is the rule in socialist countries and the exception in capitalist ones. This myth is fostered by the way in which events are reported: we read of 'communist China' and 'communist Vietnam', but not of 'capitalist Guatemala' or 'capitalist United States'; Samora Machel is always described as a socialist, but Mobutu is not 'the capitalist President of Zaïre'. It is at least implied that the communism or socialism of those concerned has a bearing on the repressive actions being reported, whereas the capitalism of others does not. Any acknowledgement of the essential relationship between oppression and capitalism would call into question the whole Western way of life, and the West prefers providing 'answers' to asking questions.

The nearest one can get to a general statement about oppression, I think, is that a country is oppressive to the degree that people are excluded from the political process. The fewer the hands holding political power, the greater the political repression. If the majority are completely excluded, as they are in both the Soviet Union and in South Africa, oppression is all-pervasive; if the majority are given some say, as they are in Western democracies, oppression is less noticeable. The reasons for the creation of power elites, of course, vary; but they all arise from the pursuit of wealth or economic advancement in the interests of either a particular group or class, or of all. The precise course that this pursuit takes, and, consequently the particular form of oppression, is, as we have noted, influenced by various historical, cultural and economic factors. If it is successfully undertaken on behalf of a group or class, that group or class also obtains political power and deliberately excludes others from an equal share of both wealth and power. If it is undertaken by a few on behalf of all, the majority are at least excluded from power. In the former case, that is in a capitalist system, the common good is not even considered; in the latter, that is in a bureaucratic socialist system, the few define the common good. In neither case do the common people have any say; in both cases the common people are neither free nor equal. One general conclusion can be drawn: oppression is the work of 'elites', consequently it will not be overcome by other 'elites', whether they be human rights organizations, political parties, governments or inter-governmental bodies.

In even the most perfectly developed form of capitalism there would be institutionalized inequality because people are not equally competitive or of equal ability. Planning is needed to ensure the practical recognition of their equality and freedom as human beings. This cannot be achieved by totalitarian, bureaucratic planning. There is no reason, however, for it not being done since, as we have seen, oppression is not natural and the restriction of individual liberty which is necessary for overcoming it does not entail the violation of anybody's *human* rights. Equality can only be achieved through some form of socialism; it can be achieved through and with freedom in a truly democratic form of socialism.

An 'elite' necessarily assumes that it knows what is best for all. But what is best for all cannot be known; it can only be continuously discovered. There is no objective, absolute common good, and it is because of this that political, and fully democratic political activity is needed. The people are best able to decide what is best for them. Elites, whatever their politics, do not trust the people; in the West in general, and in Britain in particular, they have managed to persuade a large section of the population that they are not capable of being entrusted with power and of deciding what should be done. The most they are capable of is electing representatives every four or five years and then leaving all decisions to them. Many people, as I discovered when seeking parliamentary nominations in my local constituency, have been convinced that politics is far too complicated for them and is best left to the experts. This is a guaranteed method of preventing any real change in the composition of the parliamentary 'elite', since a person stands very little chance of being nominated unless he or she conforms to the stereotyped image of the 'expert' which has been built up by the politicians themselves, aided by the media and in particular by television. But politics is mainly about knowing where you want to go; there are plenty of technicians who can work out the technicalities of how to get there. Politics is above all about ordinary people; the greatest experts therefore are ordinary people. Members of an 'elite', who share neither the experience nor the concerns of ordinary people, cannot be their democratic representatives, whether they are elected by the electoral machine, as in Britain, or appointed by the Party machine, as in the Soviet Union. They cannot re-present the interests of people if the people have no opportunity of presenting their interests.

Such elitism logically leads to totalitarianism of either the right or the left. A rightist 'elite' believes in its own virtually divine right to rule, because of superior intelligence, higher birth or greater wealth. 'The people' are simply objects of a greater or lesser degree of concern; they only become subjects when they are called upon to pay tribute to, or to vote for, the 'elite'. This process is exemplified at the Conservative Party Conference where the people cannot be entrusted with making policy decisions, but are expected to cheer dutifully. Such an 'elite' is obviously completely opposed to any form of socialism. Given even more adverse economic conditions than those presently prevailing in Britain, and increased opposition to the consequences of these, there is no ideological reason for this 'elite' not becoming as ruthlessly oppressive as the South African 'elite'.

No elite, whatever it may profess, can even want a truly democratic socialist society, since this would necessarily entail a loss of their wealth and power. A socialist 'elite' may have a role in bringing about a socialist society, if only by raising questions. It cannot, however, provide answers, since the right answer in socialist terms is the one that best meets the needs of all the people. But only the people themselves can know that. There cannot be an objectively right answer that the people are too stupid or too ill-informed to recognize. There might be economical programmes that are theoretically sound; but they cannot be part of the answer unless and until they are accepted as such by the people. To impose such programmes would necessarily involve a denial of freedom; they also would not work, since socialist programmes depend on the willing co-operation of all concerned. The task of an 'elite' or a political pressure group, therefore, is not to educate people so that they can see the wisdom of the solutions proposed by the group itself or by Marx, Trotsky, Lenin, Mao, or any other guru. Education is certainly needed, but it is education in Paulo Freire's sense; education by dialogue in which the teacher and the taught learn from each other. An 'elite' which seeks to educate from on high, to impose *its* solutions and to dictate the course which socialism should take, is on the road to Soviet-style totalitarianism.

Democratic socialism is not a middle way or a compromise between these two extremes. It is the alternative to any form of elitism or totalitarianism and is based on the greatest possible involvement of the greatest possible number of people in both economic and political decision-making. Parliamentary democracy obviously has a role in such a system; but it is not the sum total of the democratic process. It might be objected that people either cannot or, particularly in Britain, will not be responsible for such decision-making; they are not only content, they see it as their right that 'they' should do everything for them. The idea that people are not capable is part of the elitists' myth. A friend of mine in South Africa used to say that any woman in Soweto who could bring up a family on the pittance that her husband earned knew more about economics than any Chancellor of the Exchequer. That might be a slight exaggeration, but there is no reason for believing that the people who actually run a coal-mine or a car plant are not capable of having the recognized responsibility for doing so. They know how to mine coal or to make motor cars; all they might not know are those parts of the whole process that have been deliberately mystified in order to provide jobs for the 'experts'. It is not surprising that in the present system many people are happy to let 'them' take all the responsibility, since there is very little incentive for people to become involved when there are no means for them to have any real say in decisions which directly affect them.

Richard Turner, in *The Eye of the Needle*, a book which unfortunately has not been widely circulated in Britain, sketches very briefly what an ideal society in South Africa based on participatory democracy would look like:

1. The replacement of private ownership of the means of production by workers' control in industry and in agriculture. By 'worker', be it noted, is meant every individual who plays a part in the production process, from manager to cleaner. Group discussion of industrial management on a basis of equality between all these would provide the quickest way of passing managerial skills down to workers ... Initially, the bulk of the workers would probably be more concerned with wages and their own welfare, but through participation they would gradually develop the capacity to handle the more technical problems. A large-scale adult education programme communicating technical skills and explaining the operation of society would give a strong boost to this. The managerial personnel would work for three months of the year on the factory floor, to ensure that they became acquainted as rapidly as possible with the workers' perspectives and problems.

Naturally there would be no compensation paid to the previous owners, since their control of the means of production is a function either of inheritance, or of personal skill in exploiting others, neither of which ... is deserving of reward. But, of course, people like financiers, stock-brokers, property-speculators, advertising executives and absentee farmowners should be given assistance in using their undoubted skills in adjusting to a life of productive labour.

2. Workers' control of industry and agriculture would occur within the context of a political system based on universal franchise and maximum decentralization, with real powers being given to local and to provincial authorities. At each level there should be a close relationship between bodies elected on the normal constituency basis and bodies elected on an enterprise basis. This would help to integrate the common and the particular interest. The central government would keep a balance between the various regional interests, and would perform the planning functions.

The object of this scheme is not to tell people what they want, or what they ought to want. It is to give each individual the maximum possible amount of control over what happens to her/himself and hence the maximum possible amount of freedom to decide what she/he wants, and then to act to get it. Its object is to free the individual both from the direct power of others and from the power of hidden social forces. It is not a choice, but a framework within which choice becomes possible (pp. 72–3).

He adds, 'It is, I must stress, a possible society, in that there are neither imperatives of organization nor imperatives of human nature which would prevent such a society from operating once it came into existence.' I have quoted Rick Turner at length because not only was he the most lucid exponent of socialist theory that I have ever met, he was also a living example of the fact that 'love and truth are more important than possessions', a realization of which, he said, was necessary in order to be human. It is because there are people like him that one is able to retain one's belief in the possibility of an ideal society. Although he was banned, he exerted a tremendous influence on the political development of numerous people. What he said in 1972 in the book quoted and in other places is equally applicable to Britain, and anticipates much of the debate that is now taking place in Britain. (He was shot dead at his own front door in 1978 in front of his young daughter, and his murderer, not surprisingly, has not been found.)

As little more than a gesture, and also as a protest against the silencing of banned people, a group of us once decided that I should stand in the South African elections on a platform similar to that described by Rick Turner. In the event I was not allowed to stand because of my 'criminal' record. We put up another candidate, Peter Randall, who was later to be banned, and after some very hard door-to-door campaigning he received 30 per cent of the votes in an all-white Johannesburg constituency. This little experiment showed that it is not totally unrealistic to expect people to accept the idea of a fully democratic socialist system. It is not beyond the wit of people either in South Africa or in Britain to devise the actual institutions for participation in decision-making at every level from the workplace to Parliament.

Since it is obviously not possible for socialist political institutions to function within a capitalist economic framework, the most essential condition for the establishment of a socialist free and equal society is workers' control of their workplaces. That much control is not the summit of socialism; it is the beginning. In order to co-ordinate their efforts central planning at various levels is required, with appropriate democratic controls to prevent the planners becoming an 'elite' or a bureaucracy. It is not purely fortuitous that everywhere in the world there is oppression and nowhere in the world is there workers' control (Yugoslavia probably comes nearest but it is still impeded by the influence of the Party); nor that in both capitalist and bureaucratic socialist countries alike one of the main targets of oppression are trade unionists. All oppressive structures are built on control of the workers; free ones can only be built on control by the workers. That is not simply a slogan. The whole purpose of oppression, as is clear from all the examples we have looked at, is to keep wealth and power in the hands of the few. The *only* solution, therefore, is to put power and wealth in the hands of all. And the way to start that process is for workers to have control over their own labour and the produce of that labour. If it is said that this is unrealistic then we are back where we started and we have to agree with those who say that oppression is the only reality, and we can do nothing about it except sip our champagne and have abstract debates about the relative importance of freedom and equality. 'Realistic' approaches have not got us very far either in the West or in the rest of the world, and no amount of tinkering with such approaches will provide a solution. Reformist approaches are not meant to provide a solution; their purpose is to find ways of helping us to live with the problem. I do not believe in socialism as a solution; I believe in people and I am convinced that socialism provides the framework within which people can work out solutions. A solution has not and cannot be found by experts or 'elites'. The present world situation is the result of their best efforts; ordinary people could hardly do any worse. Hardened political pundits will doubtless call this naive, but even naive optimism is preferable to cynical despair. Pontificating about the complexity of problems does not help to solve them. Oppressors, too, are full of worldly wisdom and political know-how; we need something more than that to overcome the problems. Practical politics must be inspired by the political will to overcome oppression, and it is the people who have that – as the oppressors know and fear. They also have wisdom which they are deliberately prevented from expressing; the mystifying language of the pundits helps in this process.

The immediate appeal of socialism is to the poorer people in a nation and to the poor nations. The capitalist ethic has become so ingrained in Western society, and has been so effectively spread by colonialism and the continuing Western economic dominance, that socialism is often seen exclusively as a means of narrowing the gap between rich and poor or, worse, of the latter emulating the former. That much has been achieved in many countries by bureaucratic socialism, just as it has, at least to some extent, by Western capitalism; but both, as we have seen, have their price. If that is all that is expected of socialism, repression will continue in the present bureaucratic socialist states. The victims of the worst forms of capitalist oppression can hope only for a slight amelioration of their material conditions; and there is no hope of establishing a democratic socialist system in the West. There is plenty of evidence that the people who suffer under the worst forms of oppression in Latin America, Asia and Africa have seen through the capitalist myth and have realized that in order to be truly free and human it is not enough to be concerned with only material progress. They want a society in which everyone participates freely and equally. In São Paulo, where abject poverty co-exists with obscene wealth, the Justice and Peace Commission, while recognizing that 'the provision of such basic human needs as work, food, education and a roof over one's head is essential for the establishment of genuine freedom', adds: 'Unless the different sectors of the people with all their different points of view participate through their organizations, any improvement in general living standards will be eroded by bureaucracy and elitism' (São Paulo, Growth and Poverty, p. 127). It is because of what people are actually doing in face of oppression that we do not have to be satisfied with simply reforming the present system or with waiting for the experts to explain what can be done. Those who immediately dismiss the possibility of creating a free and equal society because of what people are like should look at what the oppressed are doing, not just at the oppressors.

There is more hope of creating such a society in countries which are presently grossly oppressed than in the West, where many people have come to terms with their own lack of humanity and are prepared to sell their human birthright for a reduction in income-tax. The West has very little that is positive to offer those countries. They do not need our political and economic system or even our concern for their individual rights. What they do need is for us to stop perpetuating their oppression by our support for the oppressors in capitalist countries, and by our intransigent and often misguided opposition to socialist countries, particularly the Soviet Union. I am not suggesting that we should support socialist oppressors or turn a blind eye to their repressive actions, but we should at least criticize them for the right reasons. If the West were as tolerant of the Soviet government as it expects that government to be of dissidents, there would doubtless be far less political repression in the Soviet Union and in Eastern Europe generally and the people might have the opportunity of completing the Revolution; at least the workers would not have to bear the cost of the Soviet Union's participation in the arms race and the space race, neither of which has anything to do with socialism. We could also stop impeding the efforts of the people themselves, particularly those in Third World countries, by our arrogant attempts to provide 'solutions'. This does not mean that we should adopt a 'little Englander' attitude and leave the rest of the world to solve their own problems. They are not just their own problems; they are ours too.

Because of the indivisibility of both freedom and oppression, we cannot look upon the problems from the outside, as it were, and offer disinterested help and advice. It is solidarity, not sympathy, that is required. We cannot possibly understand the problem, let alone join the search for a solution, while we believe that the problem is something separate from the West and that the solution can be found within the parameters of present Western political thought or institutions. Western capitalism is obviously part of the problem because of its direct economic and political links with even the most oppressive regimes. A reformist 'socialist' approach which would be satisfied with simply severing those links (which would be an improvement on what 'socialist' governments have done so far) would not get to the heart of the problem. We need to change ourselves and our own society – not in order to be a model for other countries to copy, but because by clinging to the basic capitalist ethic we are not only inhibiting our own development as human beings but also frustrating the efforts of those who, having suffered even more than the oppressed in the West from the effects of capitalism, are striving for a totally new society. We cannot be in solidarity with people if we are pulling, or at least giving a gentle tug, in the opposite direction. We are doing that not only if we are capitalists but also if we see socialism as nothing more than a means of getting 'more for me'.

Socialism does not mean capitalism for all; it has a different understanding of what makes people human. I was once entertained in the parlour of an English mayor, who was very proud both of his parlour and of the fact that the Council was a hundred per cent socialist. In response to his request for my opinion of his parlour, I suggested that it was rather bourgeois for a socialist Council. 'No, you don't understand,' he said. 'We want this for everybody.' Being a guest I forbore to point out that even if this were desirable, which I would not think it was, it would be impossible, since there would not be enough oak trees to provide all the panelling; and the environmental cost of providing it for some has to be borne by all.

The mayor's view is, I have discovered, a fairly typical one. It is true that if a socialist system is to distribute wealth equally it must generate wealth and must do so as efficiently as possible. It should do so more efficiently than a capitalist system does since, among other things, it should do away with costly control structures and would not have one company making a profit at the expense of another. Socialism does not make a virtue out of asceticism, but it cannot solve the problem of inequality and oppression simply by economic growth. It would not be possible for everybody in Britain, for instance, to live in the same way as the richest thirty per cent of the population presently do without damaging not only the environment but also other people in other parts of the world. It would be possible for all to have a decent standard of living if, among many other things, the rich stopped exporting £1 billion a month to countries where they can exploit people even more than they can in Britain. A high material standard of living at the cost of oppression in other countries does not make for a human existence for either the oppressed or the oppressors. A capitalist system can only keep up a pretence of being human by rationalizing oppression: capitalists do not exploit Third World countries, they are helping them with capital investments; they do not exploit workers in Britain, they just happen to be more competent and thus deserving of a higher reward. This is just as much a lie as the Soviet bureaucracy's claim to be acting in the interests of the people. To ask people to put other values and other people before material progress is not to ask them to suffer for the cause; it is to enable them to be more human. To love people and to use things is a more human and fulfilling pastime than loving things and using people. It is not possible to love both because, if having things is an ideal, then other people are seen primarily as a threat to them. One can surely derive more enjoyment from fewer things if one is aware that the more one has the higher the price that has to be paid in other people's sweat, hunger and, in extreme cases, even lives. But perhaps there are people who can only derive pleasure from perversions.

In defence of inequality it is claimed, by Hayek for example, that 'most of the strictly egalitarian demands are based on nothing better than envy' (*The Constitution of Liberty*, p. 93). But one does not envy perverts; there is nothing to envy in people who are enjoying other people's suffering. On the other hand, people cannot be expected to learn to appreciate the benefits of socialist humanness from the example of socialist ideologues and preachers who live like capitalists. The socialist message that wealth can be as dehumanizing as poverty lacks all credibility when it comes from people who themselves have more than it would be possible or desirable for all to have. The wealthy, however, do not only have more possessions than are good for them, they also have a greater share of the political power that belongs to all and a greater access to such things as education, health care, leisure pursuits, and so on. Demanding an equal share of these things has nothing to do with envying wealth. The distribution of wealth is only a means of providing everyone with what is necessary for a human existence; its possession does not make people human.

The most important thing that we in Britain can do, not only for ourselves but also for helping to overcome oppression throughout the world, is to establish a form of socialism in Britain that is both genuinely socialist (in that it rejects not only the mechanics but also the ethics of capitalism) and fully democratic, without elites of any kind. This, I am convinced, is far more important than any 'concern', however it may be expressed, about the plight of oppressed people in other parts of the world. Of course it will include real concern, but as part of an all-embracing political practice, not as a separate activity.

The Black Consciousness Movement in both America and South Africa were applying the same principle when they advised white well-wishers that the best thing they could do was to educate other Whites, not to try directly to help the Blacks, nor to decide that there was nothing that could be done. I have long been convinced that this applies also to the relationship between Britain and South Africa; I am now equally convinced that it is true in relation to oppression anywhere. When I returned to Britain I did not wish to turn my back on South Africa and not to be concerned about it, but I considered that I could best serve the cause of the people in South Africa by trying to make my infinitesimal contribution to changing Britain, rather than by trying to continue my equally infinitesimal efforts to change South Africa. People who are content with the system in Britain cannot do anything effectively to change the system in South Africa. Their well-intentioned attempts to do so by condemning its racist excesses serve only to cloud the basic issue. The two can, of course, be interrelated. Campaigning for the withdrawal of investments from South Africa, for example, has as much to do with changing Britain as it does with changing South Africa, since for as long as people are dedicated to the capitalist ethic they will not do it. There is no point in trying to make South Africa like us; the present similarity is the problem. Working for socialist change in Britain is part of the same process of working for change in South Africa and in the rest of the world. People who are involved with political solidarity campaigns are no doubt aware of this. It is those who seek to distance themselves both from the problems of Britain and from those of other countries who hinder the whole process of change, no matter how 'concerned' they may be about the unemployed in Britain or the people being killed in Guatemala.

Even in the West, and in Britain in particular, a socialist system would bring material advantages to a large number of people; but it would be to the material disadvantage of probably an equally large number. If socialism is sold to the electorate, therefore, simply as a superior economic system, it will not be bought by all and possibly not even by the majority. One response to this problem has been to water down the concept of socialism so as to appeal to the people in the middle in material terms. And so we have such compromises as state ownership of certain industries, instead of workers' control of industry, as the alternative to private enterprise. The industries are still run on capitalist lines, with bosses and workers and with the former earning up to ten or more times as much as the latter. The bosses are thus as well off, and the workers as badly off, as they would be in a capitalist system. The workers know that they would not be any better off in a capitalist system, so the satisfaction of the bosses becomes the main object of the exercise. Because of such compromises, because it is not a real socialist system, there are no effective means of distributing wealth; the neediest members of society, therefore, whom socialism is supposed to help materially, do not really benefit. Such an approach demands that the party in power, for the sake of its own stability, does not change the status quo too much. If it betrays any intention of doing so, those who have already gained some material advantage from it will switch their allegiance to another party – a party which will ensure they can hold on to what they have by not changing the status quo at all. In other words, a truly socialist economic programme is not seen by a sufficient number of people as being in their material interest for them to vote into power those recommending it, or for it to work if it were in some way to be imposed. It would be difficult, even impossible to convince them otherwise, because they might well be right in the short term.

It would be difficult but possible, I think, to convince them that a socialist economic programme within a genuinely democratic socialist political system would be in the longer-term material interest of at least the majority of the population, and in the human interest of the whole population. Marx himself maintained that socialism was in the interests of capitalists as well as of workers. Neither will be brought to a recognition of this by pretending that the present conflict of interests between the rich and the poor, capital and labour, the oppressed and the oppressors, does not exist. I see no reason why it should be necessary for conditions to become worse before capitalists can recognize the inhumanity of their behaviour and the workers can reject the inhumanity of the treatment to which they are subject.

There is plenty of evidence for those who wish to see it both in Britain and throughout the world. Many workers may be satisfied with what they have in monetary terms but, having achieved that by their own efforts, there is no reason for believing that they will remain satisfied with having to fight with management for a ten-minute tea break and with having no say in how their job is done and with how their housing estate, their borough, their city and their country are run. If we are not prepared to bestir ourselves, perhaps we will have to wait for the impetus towards socialism to come from Latin America or Africa and trust that they will continue to recognize that, even if workers do have more to lose than their chains, they still have a common interest in uniting against the oppressive, dehumanizing effects of both capitalism and bureaucratic socialism. Britain is not prepared to help the process of change in South Africa by imposing a trade boycott because of the effect this would have on the British economy. If such trade is so important for maintaining the present system in Britain, perhaps that system will eventually be changed by a black socialist government in South Africa imposing its own boycott.

Democratic socialism is also the unknown-term interest of everyone, since otherwise we might all be annihilated in the nuclear war, the threat of which arises from the worldwide conflict of interests between bureaucratic socialism and capitalism. That is the ultimate length to which they are prepared to go to protect their power, wealth and influence; but it is the logical extension of their readiness to treat people as cogs in a party machine or as labour units.

There are, of course, realists who will go to any length to resist any change in their own present, privileged 'reality'. They rationalize their position, as we have seen, by claiming that it is part of the natural order of things that some people should pay for the freedom and wealth of others. Such people will only be converted when the oppressed throw off their oppression. A more serious obstacle to the creation of a free and equal society are those who fear what socialism might mean to them, because they have been given a distorted picture of what it implies. There are doubtless many people like the elderly man at a nomination meeting who, when I said that I made no secret of being a left-wing socialist, assumed (with some anger) that if I were in power I would immediately seize the money he had managed to save after a lifetime of hard work. I had not said anything to justify such an assumption, but he had been convinced by others that that is what left-wing socialism means; whereas for me it would mean having a social system where people's needs would be properly met without having to save. In the meantime I would have no desire to raid senior citizens' bank accounts. There can, in fact, be no reason for fear, since the role of members of parliament would be that of planners and their plans could not be conceived without consultation with, nor implemented without the consent of, the people concerned. It is when politicians claim to have all the answers and are left to do what they think is best that the electorate needs to be concerned about what they might do.

Perhaps the thing people fear most about socialism is that it will reduce everybody to a grey uniformity. For the majority of the world's population even a grey uniformity would be preferable to the stark inequality which they presently have to endure. But equality does not mean uniformity. Socialism is concerned only with planning those areas of life which give rise to social conflict and which, if unresolved, lead to some imposing their will on others and thus depriving them of both freedom and equality. People's differing artistic tastes, their choice of leisure pursuits or their personal habits are not causes of social conflict and do not, therefore, need to be controlled by planning. Such reasons are, in our present system, often cited as causes of conflict; as when people claim that they do not object to their neighbours because they are black but because they do not like the smell of their cooking or the sound of their music. These are, at most, causes of personal conflict. While a totalitarian solution might be to issue an edict banning the cooking of curry in an urban area, a socialist one would be to resolve the underlying social conflict, which arises from competition for jobs, houses, etc., and to leave the resolution of the personal conflict for the individuals to deal with in the same way as they would if the cause of the offence was a white neighbour cooking tripe or playing Wagner at full volume. The purpose of socialist planning is to reduce social conflict so as to enable people to be as free as possible in other areas of their lives. Only a totalitarian state whether it is capitalist or socialist, requires total planning. In both South Africa and the Soviet Union the state interferes in the people's private lives: it decides what they can read, with whom they may associate, where they may live and, in capitalist South Africa's case, with whom they may sleep and where they may be buried.

Progress towards socialism is also seriously hindered by those who, while being anti-capitalist, set their own limits to what socialism can achieve, limits which usually coincide with their own material interests. It is really a matter of their being unwilling to go any further than of any philosophical belief about the nature of progress. For them the limits of socialism are reached in the welfare state, where the rich help the poor and the strong carry the weak. People in a welfare state, however, are still treated as objects and at best only their material needs are catered for. They are also dependent on the 'elite', of which the proponents of this view are members. Even worse, perhaps, are those who believe that the Golden Age of socialism has passed – that in Britain it reached its apogee in the immediate post-war years, and that all we have to do is get back to that.

All these reject the practical idealism without which no progress at all would have been possible and no further progress will be possible. Such idealism requires a moral base, which many people find, as some of the early socialists did, in Christianity, and others discover in Marxism or in some other conviction about the common destiny of mankind. Such a base cannot be found in a general feeling of goodwill to all men, a concern for material prosperity – especially one's own, or in a desire for power or status, or in a belief in the good of the Party. It is not, therefore, found in political careerists.

Fortunately, not everybody in Britain is a capitalist, a careerist or a 'concerned' person. It might seem a far cry from the wholesale killing of people in Guatemala to disputes within the British Labour Party. What the precise role of the Labour Party may be is not my immediate concern here; but the current debates within it do illustrate the relevance of everyday political activity in Britain to the worldwide problem of oppression. I am not referring to specific issues about elections of leaders and deputy leaders or the selection of MPs, but to the underlying principle of the need for more democracy in our political structures. This is directly relevant to what we can do about Guatemala or about oppression anywhere, because an 'elitist' party cannot create a genuinely democratic socialist system in Britain and cannot, therefore, be part of the universal struggle against capitalist and bureaucratic socialist oppression. The attempts to limit the debate to questions of party organization serve, either by accident or design, to cloud the much larger question of the need for democracy at all levels of social and political life in Britain and in the world. To treat the question in that fashion is to trivialize the most fundamental aspect of socialism. To answer it in elitist terms is to endorse the principle that underlies all oppression: that some people have more right to rule than others. There is admittedly a tremendous difference in degree, at least as far as the immediate consequences are concerned, but the principle is the same. If people cannot be trusted to run a political party they certainly cannot be trusted to run a country, let alone the world.

Democratic socialism thus becomes an impossibility. Although it is unlikely that Britain will lead the way to world socialism, we can make our small contribution to it and thus to overcoming oppression. We can only make it if we start from the conviction that it can be done – that human beings are naturally perfectable people and are not naturally possessive individuals. I have been concerned with the fact that, notwithstanding the extent and the enormity of oppression, it is possible to build a free and equal society. In working out the practicalities of how it can be done in Britain we do not ignore the plight of those who are even more oppressed than we are. We learn and take hope from the oppressed in demonstrating our solidarity with them. We recognize the point of departure and we know where we want to go; no one – least of all the self-styled 'experts' or elites – can show us the precise steps we should take to get there. We have to find the right way ourselves.

BIBLIOGRAPHY

Alves, Rubem A., *Tomorrow's Child: Imagination, Creativity and the Rebirth of Culture* (Harper & Row, New York, 1972)

Amnesty International Publications, London: Annual Reports

Torture in Greece: First Torturers' Trial, 1975 (1977)

The Death Penalty (1979)

Report on Torture (revised edition, 1979, with Duckworth)

Prisoners of Conscience in the USSR: Their Treatment and Conditions (1980)

Guatemala: A Government Program of Political Murder (1981)

Prisoners of Conscience (1981)

Report of an Amnesty International Mission to the Socialist Republic of Viet Nam (1981)

Proposal for a commission of inquiry into the effect of domestic intelligence activities on criminal trials in the United States of America (1981)

Amnesty (monthly journal)

Amnesty International, USA:

'Disappearances': A Workbook (1981)

Bailey, Martin, *Oilgate: The Sanctions Scandal* (Coronet, 1979)

Benenson, Peter, *Persecution 1961* (Penguin, 1961)

Béteille, André (ed.), *Social Inequality* (Penguin, 1969)

Brown, Peter G., and Maclean, Douglas (eds.), *Human Rights and United States Foreign Policy: Principles and Applications*, (Lexington Books, USA., 1979)

Brownlie, Ian (ed.), *Basic Documents on Human Rights*, 2nd edition (Clarendon Press, Oxford, 1981)

Commins, Saxe, and Linscott, Robert N., *The Political Philosophers* (Modern Pocket Library in association with Random House, New York, 1953)

Cranston, Maurice, *What Are Human Rights?* (The Bodley Head, 1973)

Dostoyevsky, Fyodor, *The Brothers Karamazov*, (Penguin, 1970)

Dowrick, F. E. (ed.), *Human Rights: Problems, Perspectives and Texts* (Saxon House, 1979)

Dworkin, Ronald, *Taking Rights Seriously* (Duckworth, 1977)

Fanon, Frantz, *The Wretched of the Earth* (Penguin, 1970)

Fitzgerald, Charles Patrick, *Communism Takes China* (Macdonald, 1971)

Freire, Paulo, *Cultural Action for Freedom* (Penguin, 1972)

Freire, Paulo, *Education for Critical Consciousness* (Sheed & Ward, London, 1974)

Goodman, Edward, *A Study of Liberty and Revolution* (Duckworth, 1975)

Gutierrez, Gustavo, *A Theology of Liberation* (SCM Press, London, 1974)

Hayek, Friedrich August, *The Constitution of Liberty* (Routledge & Kegan Paul, London and Henley, 1960)

Independent Commission on International Development Issues, *North–South: A Programme for Survival* (Pan Books, 1980)

Jacobs, Joe, *Out of the Ghetto: My Youth in the East End, Communism and Fascism 1913–39* (Janet Simon, London, 1978)

Kolakowski, Leszek and Hampshire, Stuart, (ed.) *The Socialist Idea: A Reappraisal* (Quartet Books, 1977)

Kommers, Donald P., and Loescher, Gilburt D. (eds.), *Human Rights and American Foreign Policy* (University of Notre Dame Press, 1979)

Lanning, Greg, with Mueller, Marti, *Africa Undermined: Mining Companies and the Underdevelopment of Africa* (Penguin, 1979)

Miranda, Jose Porfirio, *Marx and the Bible: A Critique of the Philosophy of Oppression* (SCM Press, London, 1977)

Nuttall, Jeff, *Bomb Culture* (Paladin, London, 1970)

Plamenatz, John Petrov, *Man and Society* (2 vols, Longman, 1979)

Plant, Roger, *Guatemala: Unnatural Disaster* (Latin America Bureau, London, 1978)

Power, Jonathan, *Against Oblivion: Amnesty International's Fight for Human Rights* (Fontana Paperbacks, 1981)

Robertson, A. H., *Human Rights in the World* (Manchester University Press, 1972)

Russell, Bertrand, *A History of Western Philosophy* (George Allen & Unwin, 1961)

São Paulo, Growth and Poverty: A report from the São Paulo Justice & Peace Commission (The Bowerdean Press in association with the Catholic Institute for International Relations, 1978)

Segundo, Juan Luis, *Evolution and Guilt* (Orbis Books, Maryknoll, New York, 1974)

Senghor, Leopold Sedar, *On African Socialism* (Pall Mall Press, London and Dunmow, 1964)

Skinner, B. F., *Beyond Freedom and Dignity* (Penguin, 1971)

Snow, Edgar, *China's Long Revolution* (Penguin, 1975)

Solzhenitsyn, Alexander, *The Gulag Archipelago* (Harvill Press, 1974)

Stubbs, Aelred (ed.), *Steve Biko, I Write What I Like* (The Bowerdean Press, London, 1978)

Turner, Richard, *The Eye of the Needle: Toward Participatory Democracy in South Africa* (Sprocas, Johannesburg, 1972); grateful acknowledgement is make to Foszia Fisher-Stylianou for permission to quote from this book

Williams, Roger, J., *Free and Unequal: The Biological Basis of Individual Liberty* (Liberty Press, USA, 1979)

INDEX

Philippines, 59, 84
Plant, Roger, 93, 127
Plyushch, Leonid, 134, 138
Poland, 144
Power, Jonathan, 100–101, 124ff.,
139
Prisoners of conscience, 28, 41,
46–7, 49, 150

Racism, 49–51
Red Cross, 35
Rhodesia, 31, 60, 71
Ridley, Nicholas, 83
Robertson, A. H., 26
Rousseau, J. J., 31
Russell, Bertrand, 88

Sakharov, Andrei, 131
Sampson, Anthony, 36
Segundo, J. L., 24
Senghor, Leopold, 11, 102
Small, Adam, 16, 21
Snow, Edgar, 145ff.
Sobukwe, Robert, 102
Socialism, 108–9, 131–49, 151,
155ff.
and democracy, 143, 153
Solzhenitsyn, Alexander, 130, 138,
142–3
South Africa, 10, 12ff., 56, 60, 65,
73–4, 77, 85, 119ff., 129, 131, 150,
159, 162
Soviet Union, 25, 56, 68, 73, 79,
132ff., 149, 150, 157, 162
Stalinism, 132
Stubbs, Aelred, 14
Sudan, 60

Taiwan, 52, 79, 84
Tolerance, 42, 46, 49, 52

Torture, 53ff., 64, 72, 75, 78, 87,
104, 134
Townsend, Janet, 124
Turner, Richard, 110–11, 136–7,
153–4

Uganda, 60
Unemployment, 24, 113–14
United Kingdom, 73 (see also
Britain)
United Nations, 64–78
Commission of Human Rights,
64, 75
Convention on Genocide, 65
Covenant on Civil and Political
Rights, 50, 69ff.
Covenant on Economic and
Social Rights, 69ff.
Covenant on the Elimination of
All Forms of Racial
Discrimination, 51
Covenant on the Suppression and
Punishment of the Crime of
Apartheid, 73
Declaration on Protection from
Torture, 72
Special Commission on
Apartheid, 65
United States of America, 31, 33, 73,
116ff., 126, 128
Universal Declaration of Human
Rights, 42, 48, 66ff., 76
Uruguay, 55, 70

Videla, General, 60
Vietnam, 84, 148
Vorster, J. B., 27, 67

West Germany, 116

FIND OUT MORE ABOUT
PENGUIN BOOKS

We publish the largest range of titles of any English language paperback publisher. As well as novels, crime and science fiction, humour, biography and large-format illustrated books, Penguin series include *Pelican Books* (on the arts, sciences and current affairs), *Penguin Reference Books*, *Penguin Classics*, *Penguin Modern Classics*, *Penguin English Library* and *Penguin Handbooks* (on subjects from cookery and gardening to sport), as well as *Puffin Books* for children. Other series cover a wide variety of interests from poetry to crosswords, and there are also several newly formed series – *King Penguin*, *Penguin American Library*, *Penguin Diaries and Letters* and *Penguin Travel Library*.

We are an international publishing house, but for copyright reasons not every Penguin title is available in every country. To find out more about the Penguins available in your country please write to our U.K. office – Dept EP, Penguin Books Ltd, Harmondsworth, Middlesex UB7 0DA – unless you live in one of the following areas:

In the U.S.A.: Dept DG, Penguin Books, 299 Murray Hill Parkway, East Rutherford, New Jersey 07073.

In Canada: Penguin Books Canada Ltd, 2801 John Street, Markham, Ontario L3R 1B4.

In Australia: Marketing Department, Penguin Books Australia Ltd, P.O. Box 257, Ringwood, Victoria 3134.

In New Zealand: Marketing Department, Penguin Books (N.Z.) Ltd, P.O. Box 4019, Auckland 10.

In India: Penguin Overseas Ltd, 706 Eros Apartments, 56 Nehru Place, New Delhi 110019.

Published by Penguins

117 DAYS
Ruth First

'Ruth First, who was killed by a letter-bomb in Maputo, Mozambique, on 17 August 1982, was an incisive writer, a practical academic and a creative revolutionary at the heart of the liberation struggle in Southern Africa' – *The Times*

A militant member of both the African National Congress and the South African Communist Party, Ruth First was detained under the iniquitous '90-day' law of 1963. There was no warrant, no charge and no trial – only suspicion. This is her personal account of her months in prison – her experiences of solitary confinement, constant interrogation and instantaneous re-arrest on release – lightened by humorous portraits of governors, matrons, wardresses and interrogators, seen as the tools of a police state.

'One of the most committed opponents of Apartheid, a rare person who could combine sharp incisive analysis of the system's evils with inexhaustible energy as an activist against them' – Jonathan Steele in the *Guardian*

PRISONER WITHOUT A NAME, CELL WITHOUT A NUMBER
Jacobo Timerman

Dragged from his home at dawn by an extremist faction of the Argentine army, Jacobo Timerman, the former editor of *La Opinión*, Argentina's leading liberal newspaper, was held for two and a half years – tortured, abused and humiliated – without charges ever being brought against him. Timerman's only category of guilt was being Jewish: a chilling echo of Nazi Germany and the Final Solution.

This harrowing record of Timerman's resistance, in solitary confinement, 'will come to rank with the testimony of Gulag and the Holocaust' – *The Times*

Published by Penguins

THE POLISH AUGUST
Neal Ascherson

Neal Ascherson's highly acclaimed study, now reissued with a post-script on the events of December 1981.

'This book is an attempt to describe what took place in 1980, much of which I witnessed, to analyse some of its consequences and implications, and to ask why so many hopes had to be poured away in the preceding thirty-five years' – Neal Ascherson

'Excellent and invaluable . . . The beauty of *The Polish August* is not only that he writes very well, but that he cuts through the jungle of political, social and economic issues which form the ever-tottering history of post-war Poland. What emerges is one of the most intelligent analyses available – accurate, clear, detailed and balanced' – *New Statesman*

'No-one could ask for a more lucid, sympathetic, and understanding analysis than this' – *Guardian*

SUPERPOWERS IN COLLISION
The New Cold War
Noam Chomsky, Jonathan Steele and John Gittings

As US–Soviet relations continue to deteriorate and as the arms race escalates, our outlook on world politics becomes easily confused and vulnerable to the superpowers' propaganda. Here three leading commentators cut through the myths to tackle the most basic questions, analysing the roles of the United States, the Soviet Union and China in the deepening crisis.

'If we hope to recover into our own hands the future of our own lives,' the authors stress, 'then the Dangerous Decade must become the Decade of Debate.' Informed and accessible, *Superpowers in Collision* is a vital starting-point for that debate.